# Project Sponsorship

Randall L. Englund

Alfonso Bucero

# Project Sponsorship

## Achieving Management Commitment for Project Success

JOSSEY-BASS
A Wiley Imprint
www.josseybass.com

Published by Jossey-Bass
A Wiley Imprint
989 Market Street, San Francisco, CA 94103-1741   www.josseybass.com

Jossey-Bass books and products are available through most bookstores. To contact Jossey-Bass
directly call our Customer Care Department within the U.S. at 800-956-7739, outside the
U.S. at 317-572-3986, or fax 317-572-4002.

Jossey-Bass also publishes its books in a variety of electronic formats. Some content that
appears in print may not be available in electronic books.

**Library of Congress Cataloging-in-Publication Data**

Englund, Randall L.
   Project sponsorship : achieving management commitment for project success / by Randall L.
Englund and Alfonso Bucero.
       p. cm.
   Includes bibliographical references and index.
   ISBN-13: 978-0-7879-8136-5 (cloth)
   ISBN-10: 0-7879-8136-2 (cloth)
  1. Project management. I. Bucero, Alfonso, 1956- II. Title.
   HD69.P75E537 2006
   658.4'04—dc22

                                                                    2006005267

Printed in the United States of America
FIRST EDITION
*HB Printing*   10 9 8 7 6 5 4 3 2 1

The Jossey-Bass

Business & Management Series

*This book is dedicated to three different sets of project stakeholders:*

*All the upper managers, executives, and project managers
who contributed their opinions, experiences, and practices
to this project, directly or indirectly*

*The Jossey-Bass editors who sponsored us,
who offered their commitment and support
throughout the entire project*

*Our wives, Marilyn and Rose,
who gave us unwavering support and encouragement
during the process of writing this book*

# Contents

# Preface

Who needs project sponsorship?

People come to understand different project roles by developing insight about the value of doing projects well and how people can contribute. This book is for executives or managers who are or will be sponsors of a project or program. The secondary audience is project managers, project leaders, and facilitators—the people most dependent on project sponsors to set the stage and support their success. These people need guidance in recruiting and managing their sponsors.

Many executives are assigned as project sponsors, but their organizations do not spend time training and explaining their expected roles and responsibilities during project life cycles. Thus many a sponsor, like many a project manager, ends up in the role "by accident."

Theoretically, the sponsor role can have a tremendous impact on project success. However, the reality is quite different. In our experience, the sponsor role is unclear in many organizations. Sometimes the sponsor is not very involved in the project. Sometimes the project sponsor is too involved and tries to act as a sort of super project manager, generating conflict and problems.

Management support is always needed during the project life cycle. In fact, "We need more management support!" seems to be the official slogan of a great many organizations. On every project, the project manager and his or her team needs management support. And each project needs but a single sponsor. Multiple sponsorship usually turns out to equal no sponsorship. Furthermore, to be able to give effective management support, managers need to know what is expected of them. Even worse, many sponsors do not know much about the projects they are sponsoring, and no one has bothered to explain to them the meaning of project sponsorship.

According to a study of change management research, "the number one contributor to project success is visible and effective sponsorship." Participants noted that "the top changes they would make regarding project communications in the future would be to incorporate more frequent communications earlier in the project, conduct more fact-to-face communications, *offer more communications from executive sponsors and senior managers*, and deliver more information about the impact of the change" (emphasis added). Furthermore, "many managers spend the better part of their time focusing on technology or system issues surrounding organizational changes, rather than creating a comprehensive plan to facilitate critical communications with all the sponsors and target audiences" that will be affected. Also required is to "promote visible support from executives" (Urban, 2004).

We have seen many organizations focus on the improvement of project management, the implementation of project management methodologies, and the development of a project management career path. But we have seen only a few organizations that are aware of how to develop the skills of their managers and top executives regarding the big influence they can have on project success. Graham and Englund target this audience with *Creating an Environment for Successful Projects* (2004). Dinsmore joined them to document how to implement a project-based organization in *Creating a Project Office* (Englund, Graham, and Dinsmore, 2003). Now we extend this work by focusing on the role of project sponsors within the guidelines established by our previous work. The goal is to help generate excellence in project sponsorship.

Previously, author Bucero worked as PMO manager for a multinational company that delivered customer projects. Business managers were assigned as project sponsors for the whole project life cycle. At first, project results were not very good. As manager of the project office, I got negative feedback from project teams and project managers regarding project sponsors. Project managers felt alone in front of their customers on many occasions. Then I organized a workshop meeting among the project sponsors. Conducting training on project sponsorship contributed greatly to improving the project culture. I asked questions about the level of knowledge they had regarding the projects they sponsored. The results were very significant: 70 percent of project sponsors interviewed did not possess accurate project status. Fifty percent of them never visited the project customer site. The question "What do you know and what do you not know regarding the project you are sponsoring?" elicited very surprising answers. Most sponsors interviewed did not know much about their projects. My experiences in turning this dismal situation around are revealed throughout this book. Many examples in this book describe client relationships because so much learning took place in planning and executing projects for clients. I hope you forgive me if this is not the same environment you work in; my sincere wish is that you will see some truth in the stories that you can relate to and find relevant to other settings.

Author Englund worked with many project managers and sponsors during his long career in high technology. As an author, I am fortunate in working with a cultural anthropologist (Bob Graham) who was trained to observe strange behaviors in tribes. The business tribes we studied revealed a wide variety of best and worst practices. Serving as a trainer and consultant across industries and companies offers a fabulous practice field to assess, develop, and implement more potent practices that optimize project success. Most of these efforts focus on behaviors, organizational development, change management, and executive actions. Another area of attention is creating a political plan among all management levels, addressing stakeholders who have or need a power base that deals with ever-present politics that occur in every organization. The processes and insights I share in this book derive from challenges in new product development that I faced and survived. My path led to close collaboration with Alfonso Bucero to share our experiences, identify project sponsorship as a growth need, and contribute to improving the sponsorship role wherever the need applies.

If project sponsors spend time with their project manager, project team, and customer, they will know more about the projects that are so important for their livelihood. They will be more effective and potentially generate more business. Complex projects need sponsors who are more leaders than managers. This means people who are able to establish directions for the future, communicate through vision, and create aligned high-performance teams, people who are highly focused on planning and shortening horizons. Complex projects need leaders who inspire people and fuse them into a motivated and performing team driven by a common vision.

The main purpose of a good sponsor is to add value to the project. Usually the sponsor is a person who has higher level of authority than the project manager and his or her team. The sponsor is a senior executive with business experience. Making business decisions will be necessary, and the persons who can do it best are those who know organizational strategy. But the sponsor probably needs to be taught how to be the best possible sponsor.

A good sponsor performs different functions during the project life cycle, serving as mentor, catalyst, motivator, barrier buster, and boundary manager. The sponsor is the link between the project manager and senior managers. The project sponsor is the best "project seller." The sponsor promotes and defends the project in front of all other project stakeholders.

Being a project sponsor is to be involved from project initiation to project end. Various activities are essential for project success; for example:

• During project team start-up, the sponsor develops an initial draft regarding strategic linkages and the project's vision, mission, objectives, risks, and constraints; identify the right project manager; sell the project to upper managers, team members, and other project stakeholders; and communicate the importance of the project mission.

- When the project is up and running, the sponsor works with the project manager and stays informed regarding project progress and status. Regular interaction between project manager and project sponsor is a must to talk about and decide on project issues and to learn both good news and bad. Sponsors and managers must say what they believe and do what they say they will do. Through this united front, the sponsor maintains credibility in the minds of the project team and the customer.

- As the project ends, the sponsor monitors project close-out, ensuring that the desired results have been delivered and tracked, documentation is complete, and actions have been determined for improving project processes as a result of project reviews.

- During the useful lifetime of results delivered by projects, the sponsor ensures that desired benefits are achieved that justify the investments expended on projects. Positive or negative gaps provide the sponsor with information to guide future investments.

The project sponsor also performs the role of a "change leader." Peter Senge and colleagues (1999) say, in essence, that leaders are people who "walk ahead," people genuinely committed to deep changes in themselves and in their organization. The focus in this writing is changing the level of maturity across the organization. Excellence in project sponsorship obtains better value for money spent by improving organizational maturity in defining, initiating, and managing a complex portfolio of projects. Change leaders naturally influence others through their credibility, capability, and commitment. And they come in many shapes, sizes, and positions.

In helping organizations develop PM methodologies, we have observed that many organizations do not consider the critical need for management involvement in leading change toward greater project success. The sponsor role is sometimes defined but not in depth. And that definition may be shared among project managers but not with executives. Managers are often not involved because nobody has explained to them why their involvement is important or how to improve project success.

Some managers believe that they are good sponsors because of their previous business experience. But that is not necessarily true. Some are not ready to learn from projects. Being ready to learn from every project and take action on findings is crucial for project success. Very little happens without management involvement. But managers need to know what project stakeholders expect in terms of project sponsorship excellence. Furthermore, sponsors need training in their roles and responsibilities.

Knowing that not every manager has the aptitude to be a good sponsor, it is important to choose each person in that important role carefully.

This book explains proven practices by using top worldwide companies as examples. The lessons we have learned about sponsorship in those companies are showcased in this book.

## Topics

Our concept for this book is the ascent of a staircase (see Figure P.1). Each step represents a chapter in the book; having ascended them all brings you to the highest vantage point, meaning that you see the possibilities that constitute excellence in sponsorship. All steps are necessary; some may be passed over quickly, while others are more challenging. The door at the top opens new possibilities.

Chapter One examines the role and responsibilities of a project sponsor. We examine the definition of the role and the vision and passion a project sponsor must have. We explain key lessons and how to escalate the issues.

Chapter Two examines how to obtain a project sponsor. We explain how to define criteria for getting the right project sponsor and how to sell the benefits of performing the project sponsor role. What is in it for the executive? That is the question that must be asked and answered.

Chapters Three and Four examine how to sustain sponsorship throughout the project life cycle. We explain the need to be a proactive sponsor, suggest reviews, and provide checklists. We focus

## Figure P.1  The Stairway to
## Excellence in Project Sponsorship

on how to build a strong client sponsor relationship. We explain key points in creating and sustaining customer relationships.

Chapter Five focuses on planning and running steering committees. We review how to organize those committees, take action on findings, and work together as a team.

Chapter Six helps assess client sponsorship and culture evaluation. We address issues like financial responsibilities, "owner" versus "sponsor" roles, and how to give structured feedback to the sponsor. An assessment tool is provided.

Chapter Seven deals with sponsorship execution. We explain how to establish communication channels between the sponsor and other stakeholders and the value of feedback.

Chapter Eight examines sponsorship training and development. We give a sample curriculum and provide a case study.

Chapter Nine defines the roles of mentors and mentees and explains how to set up a mentoring relationship and speak truth to power. We provide examples for implementing project sponsorship in organizations.

Chapter Ten covers two aspects of knowledge management: doing project reviews and leading with power by creating a political plan. Our concluding thoughts review the process of achieving excellence in project sponsorship and provide an overview "mind map." We provide a sample template showing how to apply the concepts presented.

A compelling case can be made for raising the capabilities of sponsors. Terry Cooke-Davies (2005) and Human Systems International conducted research worldwide to find approximately *26 percent of the variation in project success is accounted for by* variation in governance or sponsor capabilities. The capabilities that matter most: *50 percent improvement* in effectiveness when sponsors ensure strategic options are largely considered, projects are fully resourced, and project teams have the authority necessary to accomplish project goals; *70 percent improvement* in efficiency when sponsors support proven planning methods, fully develop the business case, staff capable and effective teams, and identify clear technical performance requirements that achieve business goals. Cooke-Davies concludes that "the sponsor does indeed play a pivotal role. It is time for project management professional organizations to provide help and guidance to executive sponsors!"

So who needs project sponsorship? Everyone does—on every project worth pursuing. We designed this book to serve as a key element in expanding best practices in project sponsorship across all organizations. Most chapters include tools, such as checklists, questionnaires, or templates, to assist in applying the concepts. Upper management support is a key element for creating the right environment for successful projects. We know that you will probably be following some very good practices that are not mentioned in this book. To share your practices and experiences for possible inclusion in future works, or if you have comments or questions or need assistance on anything in this book, please contact us at the e-mail addresses provided.

*February 2006*

*Randy Englund*
Burlingame, California
englundr@pacbell.net

*Alfonso Bucero*
Madrid, Spain
alfonso.bucero@abucero.com

# The Authors

RANDALL L. ENGLUND, NPDP, CBM, was a senior project manager at Hewlett-Packard and a member of its corporate Project Management Initiative team. Drawing on many years in program management for high-tech new product development, R&D, marketing, field service, and manufacturing, he now serves as an independent executive consultant at the Englund Project Management Consultancy (http://www.englundpmc.com) to guide managers and teams on implementing an organic approach to project management. He speaks, trains, facilitates, and consults across industries and at universities on improving the project environment. His ongoing purpose is to help people discover and implement ways to optimize results from project-based work. Although he completed an M.B.A. in management at San Francisco State University and a B.S. in electrical engineering at the University of California at Santa Barbara, his real education came while managing large projects at HP (twenty-two years) and General Electric (ten years).

Englund has contributed numerous articles and papers on creating an environment for project success, upper-management support, leading with power, speaking truth to power, and creating a political plan. He is coauthor, with Robert J. Graham, of *Creating an Environment for Successful Projects* (Jossey-Bass, 2004) and, with Robert J. Graham and Paul C. Dinsmore, of *Creating the Project Office: A Manager's Guide to Leading Organizational Change* (Jossey-Bass, 2003).

ALFONSO BUCERO, PMP, is now an independent project management consultant and speaker. He is founder, partner, and director of

BUCERO PM Consulting in Spain (http://www.abucero.com). He was managing director at IIL Spain for two and a half years in Madrid while also serving as a project management consultant and trainer. His background was as a project manager at Hewlett-Packard Consulting, where he developed and managed the PMO implementation whose purpose was the continuous improvement of project management discipline across the organization. During his thirteen years at HP, he managed various customer, infrastructure, development, and change management projects. He spent his last two years at HP selling and implementing the project office and convincing upper managers about the advantages of project sponsorship.

At IIL, Bucero consulted and trained executives, explaining the need for and advantages of good project sponsorship. He has a B.S. in computer science engineering, is an international project management assessor of the International Project Management Association, sponsor and then president of the Project Management Institute's Barcelona chapter, and a frequent contributor to international project management conferences and project office workshops. He is contributing editor of the "Crossing Borders" column in the Project Management Institute's *PM Network* magazine. He is the author of the Spanish book *Project Management: A New Vision* and contributed a chapter to Englund, Graham, and Dinsmore's *Creating the Project Office*.

Both authors bring a practical slant to this book—the point of view of people who have been through it all. They are practitioners of project management who share the same passion, persistence, and patience for implementing project management in organizations. They bring forth lessons that come from moving between reflection and action. They put effort into thinking about excellence in project sponsorship, leveraging best practices or inventing new ones, applying or experimenting in their fields of practice, observing and documenting the results, making modifications, and then doing it all again. This book is a product of those lessons.

# Project Sponsorship

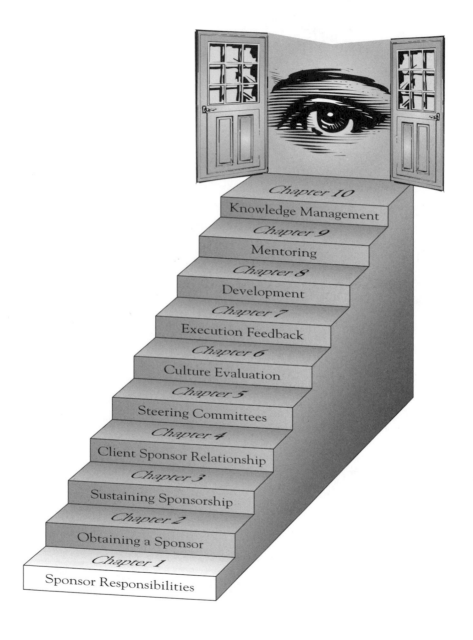

# 1

# PROJECT SPONSOR RESPONSIBILITIES

Upper managers in many organizations express frustration through statements such as "We did project management in our company, we spent a lot of money and effort training and educating our project managers, and we developed a project management career path. So why do we still have problems on our projects?"

These managers wonder when they will see improved productivity and profitability from their projects. Vendors provide software tools that appear to offer them the help they need. Conferences and seminars highlight best practices learned by other organizations, how to do portfolio management, and how to capture project requirements. Project managers earn professional certification. They learn that executive support is essential for project management to earn its benefits and enhance the practice. Why, then, do difficulties persist? We believe that an answer may lie in reviewing the organization's sponsorship skills.

This chapter defines sponsorship and identifies roles and responsibilities. We paint a broad picture of sponsorship applicable to all endeavors and then focus on specific duties that apply to the world of project management.

## Challenges

Project managers are more effective when they are *passionate* in their approach to projects and people. They need to reinforce best practices, often more than once, and explain why those methods make the most sense. To ensure that project activities get done the right way, project managers need to be *persistent*. And in taking the necessary time to talk with people and solve problems requires that they be *patient*. All three of these *P*-words may be regarded with disdain by certain managers.

Managers need to spend time with every project team member, ironing out misunderstandings, miscommunication, and varying perceptions. Managers in a sponsor role need to listen to many team members, even when the messages conveyed are not easy to receive. If you focus on people as human beings, language, culture, and unique behaviors become less of an issue. When people feel valued, they are more proactive, and performance improves. Communication is the underlying problem in many international efforts. Language differences cause difficulty, but a big issue is how different people filter directives they receive. Only 10 percent of the total message people perceive is communicated through words (Harris and Moran, 1996).

Different cultures have different values, so international team members may misunderstand the approach to executing activities and tasks that are prescribed in another country. Good managers clarify reasons for their priorities. Some multinational companies conduct initial project meetings about mission, objective, and personal roles and responsibilities, using teleconferences and videoconferences. They communicate and share information in the same way and rarely hold regular face-to-face meetings. Other companies insist that all team members get together in one place to start up a project. The project manager travels to each country where team members are located to determine  the status of activities and to observe feelings, collect inputs, and gather ideas. They give and solicit regular feedback.

Human beings adapt to the environment in which they work. A lack of cultural sensitivity distracts them from the tasks at hand. We advise all managers to understand that in a world of globalization, they must inspire project managers to advance in their understanding of other cultures and behaviors. Managers acting as project sponsors need to demonstrate their own passion to team members. All these human issues surface as sponsorship issues.

## Projects Without Sponsorship

It is perhaps easier to describe what sponsorship is not. All too often, no sponsor is assigned to a project, or the one who is assigned disappears shortly after the start and is not around when problems or conflicts appear. Some sponsors are passive; others micromanage, getting involved in every detail or decision. Some sponsors are too busy attending to other responsibilities.

Here is an example without sponsorship:

I (Bucero) managed a migration project for an insurance company while working as a project manager for a multinational services company. The project mission was to change the hardware and software platform from proprietary to open systems. My project sponsor was the general manager of that multinational company. After the proposal was signed, my sponsor took the customer general manager to dinner. At the restaurant, they talked about the importance of the project and about our know-how as providers. The customer said, "You know, we also have some software applications in our old system that would be convenient to be migrated." My sponsor said, "We have a migration center in my company, and we can migrate your applications for you." The migration took a year and a half and raised a lot of scope changes, issues, and problems.

When the project started, my sponsor told me, "Bucero, if you need me, please let me know." However, whenever I asked for more skilled resources, which I did repeatedly, I never got them. My sponsor was too busy—always traveling or otherwise occupied. It was impossible to meet him. I talked to him from time to time, but he reacted only when the customer general manager phoned him. It was very frustrating for me as a project manager and for the team members as well.

Some months later, the customer learned to live without a provider sponsor. The problem was that I had to manage all the issues and problems on my own. Many times this was very complicated. My own organization developed animosity toward me because I escalated too many issues. People would point at me and say, "Your project". . . . this and "Your project" that. I took them aside and told them, "This is not 'my' project; it is a project I am trying to manage *with your support, guys*. If you are not supporting me, the project will fail. I will not be able to do it alone." The general manager was the project sponsor, but he did not act like one, and that left a huge gap.

In this example, the sponsor supported the team during presales activities but caused trouble because he lacked technical knowledge and appreciation about the project and the difficulties generated by his inaction. He visited the customer on very few occasions. From time to time, he asked me about the project. He never read my e-mails and reports. Consequently, the project was delayed six months. When the project finally got done, the customer was happy with the efforts of the project team but absolutely unhappy with the provider project sponsor and organization.

## Case Study

CG, a banking company with offices throughout southern Spain, needed to implement new banking technology. For the new equipment to be successful, stakeholders, including CG's staff and customers, had to agree to use the technology. One company was chosen to lead organizational acceptance through application of its project management skills and processes. I (Bucero) was the project manager for that project.

After a decade of stability and prosperity, CG was under tremendous competitive pressure. Even though the company's customers were satisfied with old banking systems and methods, Y2K forced all financial entities to be prepared for disaster, meaning that they had to update or create processes, train people and upgrade, or change technology altogether. If the firm did not adapt, other banking companies would.

CG chose to implement new technology. An internal information systems (IS) strategic project consisting of functional and technological innovations appeared to answer the company's market and environmental needs.

Clear communication and intimacy with bank managers were critical success factors. The project was clearly linked to the bank's overall customer strategy, and that connection proved very helpful throughout the project. By implementing an evolved information system (from mainframe to open systems), the bank could answer its business and market needs, generate competitive advantages, increase the quality of customer service, and keep an efficient cost and profitability framework. Upper management knew it was a high priority.

Five overall factors were important for CG's project success:

- Upper management sponsorship
- A link between the project and the corporate strategy
- A quality management plan
- Communication planning and deployment
- Encouragement of the end user

The customer project sponsor had authority to make a continuous commitment to the change. He reported directly to the Bank Executive Council. I as the provider project manager spent a lot of time sharing information, thoughts, and ideas with the customer project sponsor.

The provider project sponsor, however, had little involvement in the project. He met the customer project sponsor only twice during the project. The project manager was the only real interface to the customer project sponsor. It was a difficult situation. Many times I felt closer to the client organization than my parent organization, and that created conflicts for me and my manager.

To facilitate the change, the provider shared the plan and its rationale with CG's upper managers to convince them of the plan's effectiveness. Next, we sought approval for the implementation plan from the project sponsor, and the team leader got consensus from the project steering committee as well as other stakeholders in the organization.

The provider team experienced resistance to change throughout the project life cycle. This resistance diminished, however, with personal communication among various stakeholders and by regular discussions with the customer project sponsor.

Change was imposed by the bank, but the provider had to explain the reasons and justifications for that change to each internal group. The project manager had personal meetings with each of the branch directors to clarify project goals and objectives and convince them of the major project benefits for them and for their businesses. The customer project sponsor supported all those meetings, attended some of them, and spoke with the branch directors by phone before each meeting.

The customer situation was stable in terms of processes, people, and technology, but upper managers at the bank knew that they could not ask for extra effort without any added recognition. Customer management compensated team members through bonuses.

Throughout CG, functional team leaders owned the whole project life cycle and were responsible for talking and meeting with end users, leading software development teams, and managing all tests. Leaders were trained by provider consultants to be prepared for managing and motivating their teams. The customer project sponsor spent some time every week talking to functional team leaders. These communications were crucial to the project's success.

Steering committee members also participated, not only in sponsorship tasks but also in all communications and dissemination tasks. The members talked to and supported people, boosting morale and recognizing their efforts publicly. I organized a monthly meeting with the steering committee to clarify roles, responsibilities, and misunderstandings.

Complete buy-in on the project took six months. Success at CG can be measured in terms of people, process, and technology. Defining, modifying, and using processes were some of the most difficult parts of the project, but process ownership was key. Without upper management commitment from the beginning to the end of the project, no project can be successful. The involvement and support we received from the IS manager of CG (the project sponsor) were very high. The time we spent together established a trusting relationship. Personally, it was hard for me, but I learned that to ensure a project's success, the project manager and the project sponsor must work very closely together.

This case study demonstrates that sponsorship means *commitment to people* in organizations. When we talk about project sponsors, we are referring to managers who are committed to active involvement throughout the project. These are professionals who meet regularly to track progress. One basic characteristic of a good project sponsor is to be clear about the objective and at the same time be consistent, acting as a parachute for the project team. Project sponsorship does not mean doing project planning or work directly.

Sponsorship means dealing with people. The sponsor is both a supplier and protector of resources and the focal point of escalation for the project manager. During the project life cycle, the sponsor acts as a high-level decision maker because he or she is usually more knowledgeable about the business context in which the project operates.

Sponsorship means owning the project objective, determining priorities, and keeping the project going. Many problems can be avoided on a particular project if it has a sponsor who defends the priority of the project, the project manager, and team members. For example, it is very common in organizations that provide services to customers to have conflicts in terms of resource assignments among projects. The sponsor plays a key role in that, keeping the project priority as established at the very beginning of the project. It is key for project success to have a sponsor who gives his or her team the benefit of the doubt and supports the project manager and the team.

Coaching and mentoring are desired characteristics of a good sponsor. In the project field, we do not find many sponsors who have managed projects, making it difficult for them to be effective mentors. Furthermore, they allow themselves to remain woefully ignorant about daily project obstacles, issues, and problems. Sponsorship means commitment and assuring alignment to objectives from the beginning to the end of the project.

## Sponsor Definition

There are definitions of the role of sponsor that extend beyond projects:

1. One who assumes responsibility for another person or a group during a period of instruction, apprenticeship, or probation
2. One who vouches for the suitability of a candidate for admission
3. A legislator who proposes and urges adoption of a bill
4. One who presents a candidate for baptism or confirmation; a godparent
5. One who finances a project or an event carried out by another person or group, especially a business enterprise that pays for radio or television programming in return for advertising time

Not many professionals in organizations have a clear idea of what sponsorship entails. We find different understandings and different behaviors from project sponsors across the vast variety of organizations. Some think that sponsorship is just work authorization, signing up contracts, funding the project, and deciding to go on or not go on to the next phase. Funding projects is a key role of sponsorship, but there is more.

Our definition of sponsorship is a commitment by management to define, defend, and support major activities from the start to the end.

We consider sponsorship is an active role during the project life cycle. Obviously, the types of activities to be done by the project sponsor may be different. But there are some things all sponsors have in common, including obligation, devotion, and achievement—in other words, commitment.

Usually, the project sponsor is a professional with a higher level of authority than the project manager and project team in the organization. It is preferable for the project sponsor to be an experienced executive. The person's experience is crucial to ensure that projects execute organizational strategy because the sponsor is aware of the strategy and can affect resources to support it.

## Project Roles and Responsibilities

The project sponsor, the senior manager, the project manager, and the project team all have specific roles and responsibilities.

### Project Sponsor

The project sponsor has a relationship with all project stakeholders but even more frequently with the project manager. The project sponsor performs different roles during the project life cycle: seller, coach and mentor, filter, business judge, motivator, negotiator, protector, and upper management link.

*Seller:* The project sponsor is able to sell the project to project stakeholders. The sponsor believes in the project, speaks positively about it, and can passionately sell the benefits.

*Coach and mentor:* A good project sponsor increases the level of confidence felt by the project manager. The project sponsor needs to have the ability to instill a sense of confidence in the project manager and protect the project manager from losing that confidence. The project sponsor may help the project manager understand the project business context. In this role, the project sponsor also improves the problem-solving skills and judgment exercised by the project manager. The project sponsor promotes knowledge creation and reuse of project intellectual capital.

*Filter:* The project sponsor is able to stimulate project leaders by allowing them to focus on the work at hand. The project sponsor challenges the project manager to consider more possible options and reactions but not get distracted, obliging them both to think before taking action. To be objective in assessing project relevance is an obligation for the sponsor.

*Business judge:* The project sponsor uses sound business judgment to coach the project manager when making decisions. The project sponsor is recognized as a focal point for decisions beyond the project manager's scope of authority.

*Motivator:* The project sponsor helps the project manager stay positive and solve problems with the project team. The project sponsor asks for and listens to bad news. The sponsor needs to share status and feelings with the project team about changes happening in the organization. The sponsor is present for celebrations and milestone meetings. The sponsor constantly reminds the project leader about the importance of the project mission.

*Negotiator:* The project sponsor is swift and decisive in resolving conflicts. The sponsor helps overcome obstacles that are not within the project manager's control. Obstacles may include managers who are not supportive, resource assignment problems, people problems, deadlines, lack of tools, and logistics.

*Protector:* The project sponsor works proactively with the project manager to manage risk. The sponsor is actively involved throughout the duration of the project. The sponsor keeps executives, managers, and other professionals from interfering with the team and protects the team from unnecessary bureaucracy. The sponsor demonstrates, through personal involvement with the team, that the agreed-on activities are important.

*Upper management link:* The project sponsor actively develops and manages relationships with peers in client organizations and rapidly builds trust with project managers and clients. Before establishing the project team, the project sponsor explains to the management team the project mission and objectives, the desired team, and the project descriptions. During the course of the project, the sponsor communicates to senior management and to other stakeholders. The project sponsor asks management for help and support when needed.

## Senior Manager

Senior managers have a number of obligations relevant to project success throughout the project life cycle. They delegate upper management support to middle managers in the role of project sponsor. Senior managers need to communicate periodically with project sponsors, and vice versa. Senior managers need to support and listen to project sponsors.

For this to happen, senior managers are more effective when they are clear about the objectives for each project, understand and support the project management process, and know the role of sponsors. Those things take time and commitment. Since senior managers are involved in changes that affect the whole organization, they need to assess how changes affect projects, be proactive in communicating with project teams, stay informed on project progress, and continuously review the project portfolio, both for meeting strategic goals and for necessary revisions. These activities may require additional training.

## Project Manager

The project manager is the person responsible for *getting things done*. He or she requires a proactive relationship with the project sponsor and acts at all times as the one person responsible for the project. Good project managers need to develop key skills in a number of important areas:

*Leadership:* The project manager leads the team in the use of project management methodology.

*Business judgment:* The project manager demonstrates sound business judgment in managing all aspects of a project. The manager makes quantitative and qualitative risk analyses and sound contingency plans. The project manager leads the team to achieve maximum business returns.

*Motivation:* The project manager provides a stimulating work environment and opportunities for people development.

*Effectivity:* The project manager manages overall project time-lines and is effective and timely when issues need to be escalated.

*Proactivity:* The project manager needs to be proactive in anticipating the needs of team members, the sponsor, and customers.

*Communication:* The project manager needs good communication skills and needs support to develop whatever additional communication skills may be required.

*Risk control:* The project manager deals with uncertainty and finds ways to manage and control project risk.

*Relationships:* The project manager builds relationships with all other project stakeholders.

## Project Team

Team members need to understand the high-level methodology process within the context of the project. They can identify phases, major activities, and deliverables within PM methodology. They understand and can articulate standards of business conduct.

They can describe what is legally binding and understand the project terms and conditions for the part that affects their work. They remain cognizant of customer and end user requirements as they strive to meet those requirements.

## Project Sponsor Activities

In some organizations, the project manager is selected by the project sponsor; in other companies, that selection is the result of an organizational process related to organization portfolio management. Taking into account the project characteristics and the available project managers from the organization, one professional is selected.

The project manager assignment is a formal process that gives the project manager enough authority to manage the project and also formalizes the existence of the project in the organization. The project manager needs to be respected by everyone in the organization and needs not only project management experience but also business context knowledge. It is very important that team members regard the project manager as their leader. That leader will be the link between the team and the sponsor.

An area of focus for sponsors is the start-up phase, when the most crucial decisions are made, setting the tone and pace for the rest of the project. Sponsors make a huge impact by actively participating at the start of each project. The following are some essential activities for project start-up:

- To develop a draft document with the project mission, objectives and constraints
- To identify the right project team members
- To sell the projects to executives and team members (gain commitment)
- To communicate the importance of the project's mission
- To help refine the team mission and objectives as required
- To identify deficiencies in the project plan
- To sell the project to management

## Escalating Issues

Although issue management is a project management responsibility, some issues may not be solved by the project manager and need to be escalated to somebody in the organization who has enough power or authority to do so. A wise sponsor coaches the project manager to separate technical from organizational issues and escalate organizational issues that require a broader perspective or authority to resolve. Establish a flowchart, including trigger criteria, for an escalation process.

## Sponsorship Behaviors

To implement project sponsorship in organizations means to change typical behaviors for many managers. Some sponsors suffer from less than adequate leadership and people skills; others do not know what customers need and do not see the big picture.

The "mind map" in Figure 1.1 shows desired behaviors to be implemented in organizations that want to support excellence in project sponsorship. A good project sponsor needs to deal with resource availability, minimize functional barriers, get help from upper management, and be sure the right tools are used. For example, a good project sponsor attends management meetings and project portfolio meetings and deals with maintaining project priorities. Project sponsors ensure that projects link to organizational strategy. The project sponsor role is sometimes a difficult and unpleasant job, but it is also a challenge. As each project moves forward, many issues—depicted in Figure 1.2—come up with the team, project manager, other stakeholders, and sometimes the project sponsor.

## Environment Problems

A key obligation of the project sponsor is to create the right environment for project success. When a team is in trouble, it is helpful to find out if there is any problem in the organization (crises, bad figures or results, changes)—anything that can divert the attention of team members. The project sponsor spends time explaining the importance of the project and how every team member will be part of project and organizational success.

Promoting dialogue and discussion among team members and with the sponsor helps a lot. For this reason, the project sponsor may want to attend some team meetings and gain a sense of the team.

# Figure 1.1 A Map of Sponsorship Behaviors

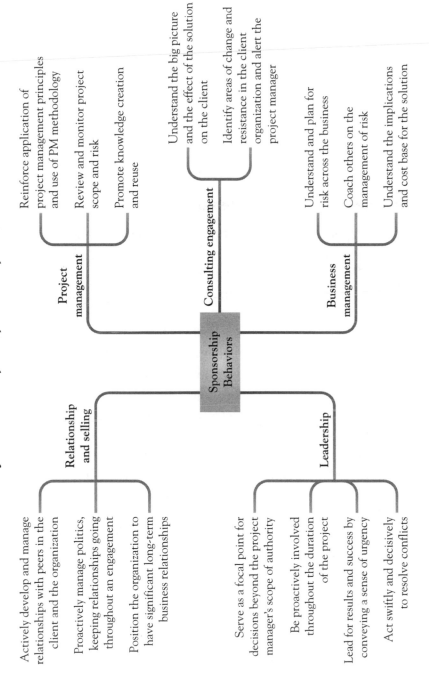

**Project management**
- Reinforce application of project management principles and use of PM methodology
- Review and monitor project scope and risk
- Promote knowledge creation and reuse

**Consulting engagement**
- Understand the big picture and the effect of the solution on the client
- Identify areas of change and resistance in the client organization and alert the project manager

**Business management**
- Understand and plan for risk across the business
- Coach others on the management of risk
- Understand the implications and cost base for the solution

**Sponsorship Behaviors**

**Relationship and selling**
- Actively develop and manage relationships with peers in the client and the organization
- Proactively manage politics, keeping relationships going throughout an engagement
- Position the organization to have significant long-term business relationships

**Leadership**
- Serve as a focal point for decisions beyond the project manager's scope of authority
- Be proactively involved throughout the duration of the project
- Lead for results and success by conveying a sense of urgency
- Act swiftly and decisively to resolve conflicts

## Figure 1.2   Typical Sponsorship Problems

| Project sponsor problems | | | Environment problems |
|---|---|---|---|
| | Common Problems and Issues of the Project Sponsor | | Team member problems |
| Problems with others managers | | | Project manager problems |

## Problems with Team Members

Project sponsors can be helpful in a number of ways.

• *Project sponsors can ensure that project team members attend project meetings.* Missing team meetings may cause team productivity problems and lead to more problems for the rest of the team, lack of motivation, and low morale. The project sponsor is best advised to deal with the problem immediately, talking to each person who misses a meeting, finding out the causes, and ensuring resolution. Teamwork is crucial for project success.

• *Project sponsors can protect team members from serious conflicts.* Sometimes the stress of project work or other circumstances generates conflicts between two or more people. The project sponsor can ask individually about the causes of the conflict and try to resolve it.

• *Project sponsors can keep the team from becoming too dependent on the sponsor.* Some teams need too much direction from the project sponsor. This usually happens when the organization has an autocratic management style. The project sponsor needs to delegate sufficient authority to the project manager.

• *Project sponsors can prevent team conflict during presentations.* Sometimes team members have different opinions or arguments regarding project activities and execution. If during management presentations, some of them seem to not fully support recommendations, fall apart, or argue about their differences, the project sponsor may need to facilitate more effort on teamwork and motivation.

- *Project sponsors can make sure that team members do not skip steps.* In some projects, the team skips actions or tasks in the project plan or does an inadequate job. Sometimes this is because the project manager lacks authority. In that case, the project sponsor needs to reinforce the power and authority of the project manager within the team, as well as support following the PM methodology.

- *Project sponsors can keep team members from becoming dysfunctional.* A team member can disrupt teamwork and team progress during the project life cycle. Project managers usually deal with that situation first, but if the manager is unable to solve it or tarries too long, the issue needs to be addressed by the project sponsor.

- *Project sponsors can keep the team moving.* When the project manager acts to speed up a slow-moving team but fails, the project sponsor may want to organize a meeting and investigate the circumstances.

- *Project sponsors can prevent stalemates.* The project sponsor supports the project manager to choose the best people available. However, getting the right people is not always possible, and some projects do not make progress, even after meeting and brainstorming. In that case, the project sponsor and project manager need to talk, find out what the obstacles are, and develop a different approach before meeting with the project team again. The reason may require unseating false expectations and creating clear stakeholder expectations. It may mean rescoping the project to match the resources and time available.

- *Project sponsors can prevent meeting interruptions.* A best practice for the project leader, with support from the sponsor, is to ask each member to accept accountability for meeting success and discipline in following effective meeting processes. Mobile phones should be turned off. People should commit to the whole meeting and be actively engaged. The first person who should set the example is the project sponsor.

- *Project sponsors can make sure that the project's mission and objectives are validated throughout the project life cycle.* This means that the project sponsor clarifies the desired specific achievement and answers questions that may arise. The sponsor has a key responsibility to keep the team on track and to handle changes when they are mandated by circumstances or strategic shift or when progress (or lack thereof) suggests that the objective may need modification.

## Project Manager Problems

Project sponsors may have to deal with some of the following scenarios:

• *Project manager avoids project sponsor:* Sometimes the project manager does not understand the role of project sponsor or does not want to be available for meetings with the project sponsor. In some cases, the project manager feels intimidated by the project sponsor; at other times, the project manager is uncomfortable in that role or is afraid of reporting negative behaviors from a team member. Sometimes there is a communication problem or a chemistry problem. Although it is a requirement of project management to work well with people, not all project managers and project sponsors can understand each other. Believe it or not, even some sponsors are very difficult to work with.

• *Project manager in the middle:* The project manager feels bad because the team is heading one way and the project sponsor wants something else to happen. Sometimes that situation is also a communication problem. The project manager and project sponsor need to agree on and clarify all project objectives. The project manager has a role to create teamwork and motivation from the beginning of the project. In order to help, the project sponsor needs to create and support an open, trusting atmosphere among project manager and team members.

• *Project manager not working out:* It may be that the wrong manager was assigned to the project. In many companies, there are no established criteria for project manager selection. Accidental project managers—those assigned at random or because they happened to be at the place at a certain time or made a suggestion—are not prepared for the job. Sometimes technical experts are assigned as project managers, and they do not like to deal with people.

- *Project manager burnout:* The project manager's spirit is going down because he or she is overloaded or has a poor relationship with the project sponsor or team (or both) or does not receive sufficient support from the sponsor.

## Problems with Other Managers

Sometimes, mainly in non-project-oriented organizations, we find three types of difficult managers: *unsupportive managers* who refuse to allow employees to attend project meetings, *sabotaging managers* who undermine the team's mission, performance, or recommendations, and *threatened managers* who are upset that employees are meeting with upper managers and the project sponsor.

## Project Sponsor Problems

Project sponsors can cause problems too. Project sponsors tend to use certain styles of management that are ineffective or inappropriate:

- *Tendency to overcontrol:* The project sponsor acts like a super project manager. Sometimes this is a management style. At other times, the project is very critical and the project sponsor is nervous or uncomfortable.
- *Proximity:* The project sponsor stays too close to the team or too far from the team. For example, the project sponsor attends all meetings and asks too many questions of all team members. Or the project sponsor attends the project start-up and management meetings but does not display interest in the project's day-to-day issues. Or the sponsor is virtual, residing at a distant location.
- *Lack of time:* The project sponsor is not able to spend time supporting the team by meeting with the project leader, is unable to attend team meetings, or is too busy with other activities.
- *Manipulating the team:* The project sponsor believes that he or she knows the right team approach or plan and influences the team to do only what he or she wants.

- *Not sharing:* The project sponsor does not believe in the team and refuses to share thoughts or ideas, assuming that the team must explore everything from scratch.

## Tools

Tables 1.1, 1.2, and 1.3 reflect three different approaches to the sponsorship role. Table 1.1 is based on the Project Management Body of Knowledge (PMBOK) (Project Management Institute, 2004), Table 1.2 is client-based, and Table 1.3 is for new product development. Each provides a proactive basis for creating an effective project environment and avoiding problems.

## Summary

Project success can be ensured through better project sponsorship. Sometimes executives are unable to pull the plug on "ill projects." Yet all the resources, energy, and passion not poured into those "ill projects" could substantially improve the company bottom line. Project sponsors fulfill a crucial role by guiding right decision making throughout the project life cycle.

Executives are advised to support project management in organizations in order to reap the benefits. This means they need to spend time understanding their roles and responsibilities during project life cycles. Sponsorship means dealing with people. Unfortunately, many professionals operate without a clear definition of sponsorship. Sponsorship requires taking an active role during the whole project. Serving as the project sponsor requires making a commitment to define, fund, defend, and support major activities from the start to the end.

As explained in this chapter, the project sponsor has a relationship with all project stakeholders, especially the project manager. The project sponsor performs various roles (such as seller, coacher, and mentor) during the phases of each project. Many of these roles require that new skills be developed. That takes time.

**Table 1.1  Roles Under PMBOK-Based Sponsorship**

| Sponsor Activities | Project Management Deliverables | Initiation Process Group | Planning Process Group | Execution Process Group | Control Process Group | Close Process Group |
|---|---|---|---|---|---|---|
| Project initiation | Project charter | E | | | | |
| Scope review | Preliminary project scope status | R/I | R/I | R/I | R/I | |
| Getting informed | PM plan | R | | | | |
| Getting informed | Deliverables | | | I | I | I/A |
| Review request | Requirement changes | | | I/R | I/R | |
| Is informed | Work performance information | | | I | I | |
| Is informed | Approved change request | | | | | |
| Is informed | Rejected change request | | | | I/R | |
| Review with PM | PM plan updates | | | | I/R | |
| Review with PM | Project scope status updates | | | | I/R | |
| Is informed | Performance reports | | | | I/R | |
| Is informed, reviews, and shares | Forecasts | | | | I/R/S | |
| To be informed | Administrative closure | | | | I/A | |
| To be informed | Contract closure | | | | | I |
| Approves and is informed | Project acceptance | | | | | I/A |

Note: E = execute, R = review, I = inform, A = approve, S = share.

## Table 1.2  Questions to Be Answered
## When Contemplating Client-Based Sponsorship

*Understanding the Client*

- What is the business condition?
- What are the account's major products and services?
- What is the company's position in the marketplace?
- What are the business objectives of this account?
- What is the account's industry climate?
- What is the account's position in the industry?
- Who are the major or key clients of this client?
- What is the account's IT environment and installed base?

*Understanding the Deal*

- What are the client's business needs for this project?
- What are the requirements and client expectations for this project?
- Is the project in line with or part of the client's strategic plan?

*Influencing the Solution*

- Are we driving the solution planning and design as a trusted adviser?
- What is the differentiation of the proposed solution based on?
- What are the needed presales resources and related costs?
- What is the total presales time?

*Understanding the Provider Profit and Risk*

- What is the calculated monetary risk in this deal?

*Pursuing the Deal*

- Can the provider establish a sales presence with reasonable investment?
- What is the financial condition of the account?
- Are funds designated in the client's budget for this project?
- What is the provider's business potential in this project?
- What is the level of client competence in this project?
- Does the client have a clear driving mechanism for the buy?
- What is the strategic marketing value of this project?

*Fitness to Compete*

- What is the provider's position in the client relationship?
- Why does the client want to do business with us?

*Positioning to Win*

- Does the deal team have access to the client's upper management?
- What is the sales objective?
- What is the selected sales strategy?
- What is the plan to compete against a suspected indirect counterstrategy?
- What is the tactical plan to close the deal?

*Resources*

- Is a steering committee required?
- Are required project team members available?

**Table 1.3 New Product Development Process**

| Phase 0 Requirements and Planning | Phase 1 Study and Definition | Phase 2 Specify and Design | Phase 3 Development and Testing | Phase 4 Pilot Testing and Prep | Phase 5 Enhancement and Support | Phase 6 Maturity |
|---|---|---|---|---|---|---|
| **Phase Exit Objectives** | | | | | | |
| Describe specific requirements consistent with business and technology plans | Define the product; integrate the product into functional strategies | Identify and commit resources; design the product | Develop the product | Test the product; prepare for shipment | Support the product; complete product enhancements | Maintain the product; discontinue the product |
| **Complete Activities or Deliverables at Phase Exit** | | | | | | |
| Product and market requirements complete | Product specifications complete; product schedule and interdependencies determined | Design specifications complete; functional plans complete; design released | Functionality complete; prototype signoff | Product, certification, and user testing complete; product released | Production and sales objectives met; enhancements implemented | Discontinuance plans implemented; CPE complete |
| **Sponsor Commitments at Phase Exit** | | | | | | |
| Fund and staff product study; identify vision and constraints | Fund and staff product design; validate product objectives | Fund and staff product development, testing, and support; validate product plan | Decide on price, performance, availability, and product manufacture | Authorize unrestricted customer shipments | Support current product engineering | Provide specialized support |

Sponsor activities and behaviors vary with the organization. The lack of good project sponsorship is a major case of difficulties and problems on projects. Well-executed sponsorship by senior executives brings better project results.

The key lessons are these:

- The absence of thoughtfully assigned sponsors with well-defined and clearly understood responsibilities is a major cause of project difficulties and frustrations.
- Complex programs that cross internal and external organizations require a structured approach to sponsorship.
- Senior executives are more effective when they understand their role as sponsors and do not delegate this responsibility to lower levels.
- Well-executed sponsorship brings financial results, increases motivation and participation, and improves the impact of project-based work on the organization.

A good project sponsor needs to deal with resource availability, minimize functional barriers, get help from senior management, and be sure the right tools are used. A key obligation of the project sponsor is to create the right environment for project success. Problems and issues that arise from people working on projects are greatly eased when effective sponsors are fully present and skilled in fulfilling their roles. The rest of this book addresses how to make this happen.

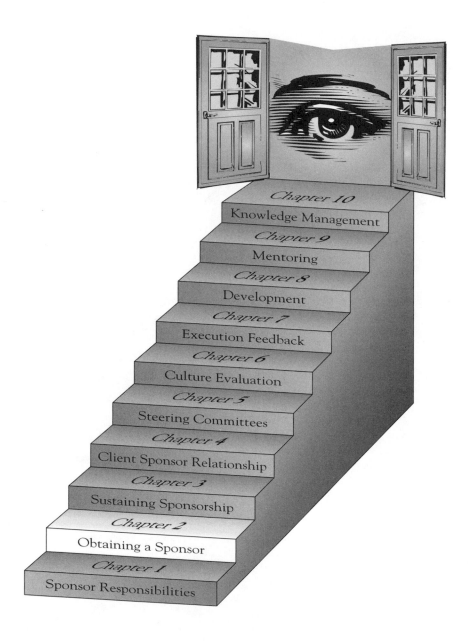

Chapter 10
Knowledge Management

Chapter 9
Mentoring

Chapter 8
Development

Chapter 7
Execution Feedback

Chapter 6
Culture Evaluation

Chapter 5
Steering Committees

Chapter 4
Client Sponsor Relationship

Chapter 3
Sustaining Sponsorship

Chapter 2
Obtaining a Sponsor

Chapter 1
Sponsor Responsibilities

# 2

# OBTAINING A
# PROJECT SPONSOR

Courage is resistance to fear, mastery of fear—not
absence of fear.

—*Mark Twain*, Pudd'nhead Wilson

Upper managers are the arches of a project cathedral. Sweeping, powerful arches support vast cathedral construction and are required to be present for the full length of the structure—from the beginning to the end. The same is true for project sponsors and how they contribute to project success. Complex projects need sponsors who are more leaders than managers. Leaders establish directions for the future, communicate through vision, and forge aligned high-performance teams. In contrast, managers focus on planning and short-term horizons, devise processes and structures, and solve problems.

Much as cathedrals create inspiration, projects need leaders who inspire people and fuse them into a motivated and performing team driven by a common vision. When senior managers act as sponsors, they provide support and passion to managers and the rest of the project team.

This chapter addresses the questions about why persons choose to sponsor projects, what is in it for them, what characteristics they possess that make for excellence in sponsorship, and how to get these people to sponsor projects. Cathedrals are built because someone has a grand vision that he or she wants to turn into reality; it then requires mustering the means to make it happen. Sponsorship is that force.

## Why Choose to Sponsor a Project?

We asked this question of project professionals worldwide. Here are some answers:

Marcus Funke, PMP, says, "Whoever takes on sponsorship of a project will be affected by the outcomes." He notes that on the plus side, visible success results in recognition and visibility for the sponsor. But failure of the project, or even "horror stories" about the project, leave a "bad taste" and have various negative side effects on sponsors. Some of these effects may never be officially articulated, but delayed promotion or "career freeze" . . . may be a consequence.

A sponsor typically evaluates these potential side effects when selecting a project. For example, sponsors may use the project like a chess piece to play "strategic business games" and improve their recognition and visibility. They may use the project to bolster their business success in an important area. They may use the project as a weapon directed against other projects, in internal "power plays" to get rid of competitors. And if they are appointed to the position, they may try to avoid being known as the sponsor if they do not believe in the outcome.

Alessandro Difazio, a project professional from Italy, has been handling software engineering and offshore activities for an Italian consulting organization. He has been involved as a project sponsor or "appointed manager," as they call this role in his project environment. His answer to why sponsor a project? "To be sure the project will be instrumental to the overall strategy the sponsor is responsible for." Success then serves as a testimonial for the rest of the organization about the sponsorship role.

Project professionals' reasons can be classified in four distinct categories:

- *Business reasons*—the project can be completed successfully within the proposed schedule, scope, and resource bounds.
- *Political reasons*—the value of a successful project is worth the investment and the risk of failure.

- *Personal reasons*—to sponsor this project is a professional challenge for me. I want to improve my skills in dealing with people and organizations and learning to make the right decisions.
- *Stakeholder reasons*—the other project stakeholders want me as the sponsor. They believe that I have sufficient power and influence, knowledge of the business, and leadership skills to do a good job.

Achieving excellence in sponsorship means that senior managers get to maintain a hands-off approach but are available when problems come up. Senior managers expect to be supplied with accurate project status reports; their position as sponsors gives them a firsthand view of project status. They can be close enough to understand the issues and get direct feedback on how systems are working. They extend their influence in the organization when they empower people and decentralize project authority. They do not have to solve all problems themselves because they expect project managers and their teams to suggest alternatives and solutions.

The right project sponsor is able to empower the project manager and the team and give them the benefit of the doubt. This means being tolerant of mistakes. People learn from mistakes. People sometimes need to be wrong in order to change their ways. This learning process also applies to sponsorship. Selecting the right project sponsor is not an easy task, and many organizations do not have a process established to help them do it well.

## Criteria

The project sponsor needs to be a change leader. "In essence, leaders are people who 'walk ahead,' people genuinely committed to deep changes, in them and in their organization. They naturally influence others through their credibility, capability, and commitment. And they come in many shapes, sizes, and positions" (Senge and others, 1999, p. 19).

Having enough trust and belief to pursue a vision is what signals to others that the vision is worth investing in. However, it is usually actions, not words, that send the message. The best sponsor is somebody who understands his or her role, believes in the team, and wants to execute the role.

The project sponsor is usually an upper manager who, in addition to his or her usual responsibilities, provides ongoing support to one or more specific projects. Often middle managers are tagged to be project sponsors because senior managers tend to be very busy and so they delegate the sponsor role. This practice usually does not work well. Those middle managers very often cannot do a good job because they do not have enough power and authority to execute it.

Although project sponsorship is always needed, not all projects need a formal project sponsor assigned to them. Organizations need to make a decision about what projects in their project portfolio should have a project sponsor. One guideline is to set threshold criteria such as a major customer commitment, projects over a certain size in terms of money or resources, or new product or technology versus a patch or minor enhancement. If there is a question as to whether or not to assign a sponsor, it is wise to err on the side of doing so.

Some organizations believe that it is impossible to assign a senior manager to every project, so they create a "sponsorship committee." That committee may be a business team formed by representatives from different functions of the company. It serves as a "sponsor organism" for many projects. The committee assigns the project manager and team for every project as part of the project charter development process. During the project life cycle, the committee addresses strategic issues and schedules project reviews with the project managers. A problem with this approach is that team members or other project stakeholders do not build rapport or consistent experience with an individual and do not know whom to go to when they have issues to escalate. On the other hand, they may have many resources to go to when a primary contact is not available. This committee approach seems to work well only in mature project-oriented organizations.

The criteria for selecting a project sponsor depend on the project culture of the organization. Look for the following qualities in potential project sponsors:

- They feel the need for change; they are not satisfied with the status quo.
- They believe that the effort to change the situation is more attractive than business as usual.
- They have vision—a clear and articulated picture of a desired performance.
- They are consistent in their actions, activities, and reactions.
- They are willing to invest time and energy; they care and feel they have a vested interest in the outcome (*skin in the game, se dejan la piel*).
- They place a high priority on the value of project-based work and the outcomes produced.
- They have a perspective on the future.
- They believe that things can be improved when effort is put into learning from experience.
- They are capable of making a realistic appraisal of resources; they have a complete understanding of the time, money, and people required for the project.
- They have empathy.
- They are able to anticipate customer needs.
- They have power within the organization.
- They understand the business and how things get done in the organization.
- They are publicly and privately supportive.
- They can manage consequences because they know the project environment and the organization very well.
- They follow the progress of the project.

A key criterion is that the person is interested in and wants to be a sponsor. Our recommended approach is to *ask* the candidate if he or she wants to be the sponsor for a particular project.

Good sponsors are usually unable to sponsor more than one project at a time. On IT projects, the project sponsor can expect to spend 10 to 25 percent of his or her time supporting the project.

## Selling Sponsorship

Although upper management support is repeatedly cited as a critical success factor, this does not necessarily mean that the organization fully understands and supports project sponsorship. Like most other practices, project sponsorship needs to be "sold." Individuals fulfilling the sponsor role need to be sold on the features, advantages, and benefits that result from excellence in sponsorship. Then they need training in the roles and responsibilities of a sponsor. They also need continuous feedback on how they are doing.

The sponsor adds value to the organization because the sponsor, as an executive, knows the organization, knows the business environment, and is in the best position to help the project manager manage the project successfully. The sponsor role is decisive and has a major impact through the business decisions that the sponsor makes.

The sponsor adds value to the project manager and project team by supporting them and defending them in front of the customer and the organization. The sponsor knows how to speak the language that other managers and investors understand.

The sponsor adds value to customers—listening to them, making decisions, and helping all stakeholders consider what is best for project success. The point is how to sell the project management story to senior executives. An answer is to identify and emphasize the few key competencies of project management that can transform organizations. Translate the message into a story that is easily understood.

Selling the need for project management to executives is one of the most important steps in the implementation of organizational project management practices. Executives will be project sponsors who know the meaning of a project and the implications to support them. Talking to project managers around the globe confirms that to gain a "go" decision from executives requires a successful three-step selling model that we call APF (for *assess, plan,* and *follow*). This method to gain upper managers' support is the result of the experiences of project managers in the field who have successfully implemented project management in their organizations with the blessing of their executives. Organizations are more effective when they recognize excellence in project sponsorship as a core competence.

## The Sponsorship Selling Model

The model for selling sponsorship (see Figure 2.1) breaks down into the following steps:

*Step 1: Assess.*   Understand the need  for a sponsor for your project.
   • *Understand the need.* Focus on the organizational need for a project sponsor. Each level in the organization will have a list of priority needs. The best way to cover executive needs is to understand the key strategic priorities for the organization. This could be accomplished through periodical reports, discussions with senior executives, or meetings. Make strategic priorities, goals, and objectives explicit, and see where your project fits and how important it is for the organization.
   • *Assess your environment.* Then select a sponsor who will be most affected by the benefits and value produced by the project (an environmental assessment survey instrument (EASI) serves as a systematic questionnaire covering the ten components of an environment for successful projects; see Englund, 2004a).
   • *Find the right sponsor for your project.* This is typically someone who is responsible for a critical business unit, someone who can make an impact on the business and has the authority to do so and the visibility to gain support. If this same individual was also responsible for troubled projects in the past, it will even be easier to

## Figure 2.1 The Sponsorship Selling Model

- Understand the need of a sponsor for your project.
- Assess your environment.
- Identify who would be the right sponsor for your project.
  - Business impact
  - Authority
  - Visibility
- Meet your potential sponsor, and say, "I need your help."
- Share your thoughts with other managers and do a SWOT analysis.

**1. Assess**

**Sponsorship Selling Model**

**3. Follow**

- Keep your sponsor updated periodically. Anticipate good and bad news.
- Speak about the advantages of working together in different meetings.
- Establish a strong relationship.
- Share and communicate the advantages.

**2. Plan**

- Involve the selected executive (sponsor) in the project scope definition.
- Develop and share a communication plan with your sponsor.
- Prepare a business case.

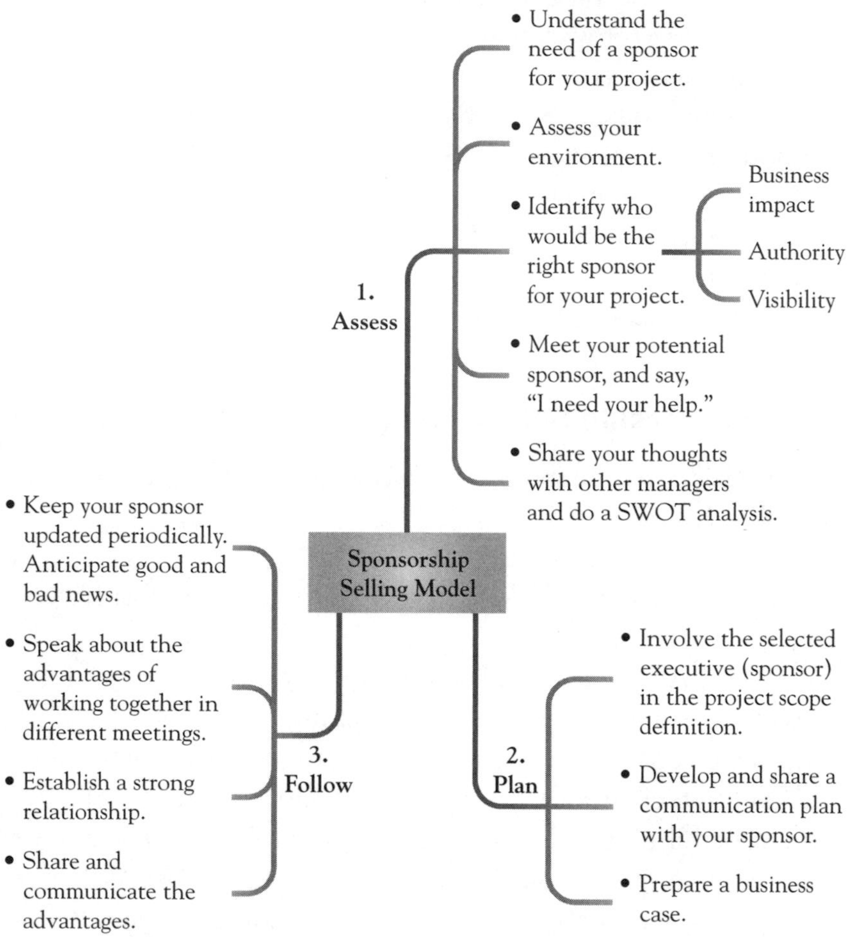

gain his or her support when you can relate to those projects and explain how a strong relationship between the sponsor and the project manager can produce greater business impact.

- *Meet your potential sponsor and say, "I need your help."* There is no substitute for a face-to-face meeting between people to share concerns and ask for assistance.

- *Share your thoughts with other managers in the organization.* Always speak about the project and its business impact, not about yourself as a project management believer. Ask the management team for consensus about getting a sponsor assigned to your project. Assess strengths, weaknesses, opportunities, and threats, especially with regard to relationships between the sponsor and other stakeholders.

*Step 2: Plan.* Involve your assigned sponsor from the very beginning.

- *Involve your sponsor.* Talk about his or her expectations and your own expectations. Relate that the project sponsor can help the project manager and his or her team achieve a big business impact throughout the project. Brainstorm about what, how, and when the sponsor's involvement will be necessary and his or her interactions with the project manager. One key involvement is achieving consensus on project scope definition.

- *Develop and share a communication plan.* Communication with business leaders and others in need of project management is often forgotten. Continually remind people of the value and capabilities contributed by project management and the willingness of your group to help the business units meet their goals. Include the target audience, frequency and type of information presented (issues to be mitigated, escalation process, progress updates, capabilities and benefits). Advertise and communicate—that is how to sell sponsorship.

- *Prepare a business case.* Complete a business case with all key business unit personnel. Producing the business case as a team will help get buy-in from all departments involved and the upper managers. This business case is a valuable selling tool for gaining funding approval.

The business case includes:

- Key business challenges, goals and objectives to address
- Proposed sponsorship strategy—approach, expectations, project resources
- Benefits and value project sponsorship will bring to the organization
- Proposed cost
- Rollout plan

The secret to selling an executive is to focus on the primary business needs and the value sponsorship can bring to the organization. The primary business needs come from the first step (understanding the need). The two key value items that executives want to focus on are how project management can reduce costs and how project management will increase revenues or better fulfill the unit's mission.

*Step 3: Follow.*  Talk to your sponsor frequently.
- *Keep the sponsor updated.* Schedule periodic meetings to talk about the project. Anticipate good and bad news; adopt a practice of keeping management informed so there will be no surprises.
- *Talk about the advantages of working together.* Help the sponsor understand that by working together, he or she will know much more about the project and about the customer and will consequently be more valuable to the organization. Use management meetings to reinforce and underline the support and help of your sponsor.
- *Establish a strong relationship.* Project success is all about people working together. Strong relationships are as important as tasks and often more so.
- *Share and communicate advantages.* Be the constant evangelist who helps others see the good that can come from exellence in project sponsorship. Explain the value of this approach to all managers.

## Rewards for Project Sponsorship

What will the sponsor get in return? This question is crucial and needs to be answered, both by teams requesting a sponsor and by individuals contemplating accepting the role. When we asked a former CEO of Hewlett-Packard how the Project Management Council could be more effective across the company, he advised the corporate Project Management Initiative to get an executive sponsor. Nobody quite knew what this meant. It was easy to begin defining what that person could do for the project management discipline. We took pause when asking the question about what would be in it for an executive to take on this new, voluntary role whose value was uncertain.

An answer usually depends on each project. The benefits of being a project sponsor can be sold to sponsors. Certain benefits have been repeatedly demonstrated:

- An improved standing and profile within the organization. Important projects may empower project sponsors to success (but also may destroy them in case of failure).
- Being linked with an exciting and very successful project. Exciting projects have high visibility in organizations.
- Marketing potential for the project sponsor (image selling). The assignment was a reflection of the sponsor's professional background and prestige.
- Greater popularity. Media opportunities at official launches, presentation evenings, and mentions in local newsletters or news gain wider exposure.
- Easier agenda implementation. Sponsorship represents an opportunity to turn a vision into reality through a set of assigned resources.

Never underestimate the power of simply asking potential sponsors what they want from the experience. They may cite interests that would not have surfaced had you not asked. Dialogue is a powerful investigative tool.

Selling sponsorship is a sales process. To build your sales presentation, follow these steps:

1. *Align.* Know your executives extremely well. Gather insight into their values and ambitions. Put yourself in the shoes of these persons to understand the forces that drive them.
2. *Build.* Define what sponsorship means in your organization. What do you expect from your executives as sponsors? Build a relationship with them.

3. *Demonstrate*. Emphasize the value of sponsorship and the advantages that accrue to business when it is done well. Ask your sponsors what they know and what they do not know about the projects they are involved in. This is not meant to reveal ignorance but to get their attention.

4. *Close*. Get executive commitment. Get an agreement about next steps (action plan).

## Negotiation

When a senior manager is assigned to sponsor a project, the manager expects something in return. To be a good sponsor is not enough for project success; there are too many unpredictable elements in the project environment that can cause project failure. Project sponsors take a risk when they accept the role, but it is also a challenge for them to be recognized as the "strategic driver for project success."

Sponsor assignment negotiation needs to present it as a win-win situation. If the project sponsor does not feel comfortable with the role, the project manager and team will run into difficulties during the project. Allow the person the opportunity to question, explore, research, and bargain before accepting the responsibility.

Sometimes sponsors are not selected according to any rhyme or reason; they are assigned regardless of their capabilities to do the job. This is not a recipe for success. Take these four basic principles for negotiation into account:

1. Separate people from the problem, the relationship from the matter of the negotiation. Try to view the situation from the other's person perspective, and provide opportunities for both of you to express your emotions. Pay attention, listen, and do whatever you can to build a working relationship.

2. Focus on interests, not positions. You know your interests, the ones that have caused you to take your position. Now try to

figure out the other parties'. Acknowledge their interests; give the people on the other side positive support equal in strength to the vigor with which you emphasize the problem.

3. Invent options for mutual gain. Then broaden your options, looking for room to negotiate. Look for mutual gain by identifying shared interests. These opportunities exist in every negotiation. Stress them to make negotiations smoother and more friendly. Make the other person's decision easy. Look for possible agreements early in the process. Float trial balloons that point toward areas of closure.

4. Insist on objective criteria. That takes advance preparation and evaluation of alternatives. Frame each issue as a joint search for objective criteria, as if you assume that the other party is doing the same thing. Reason soundly, and be open to reason. But yield only to principle, not pressure. When you feel pressure, invite the other person to state his or her reasoning. Then suggest objective criteria, and refuse to budge except on this basis. Get closure.

## Informing

The formal way to authorize a project is through the *project charter*. It documents updated project information for use by all project stakeholders, identifies the sponsor and project manager roles, and gets the project acknowledged by the organization.

In a video clip on the CD *Understanding Project Management* (Strategic Management Group, n.d.), Bob Graham describes how, as a consultant, he came into a financial services firm and within minutes was able to distinguish successful from unsuccessful projects by a quick review of project charters. The successful projects had a sponsor's name clearly identified. Unsuccessful projects had a blank listing or no specific person for the sponsor.

A project initiator or sponsor external to the project organization, at a level that is appropriate to funding the project, issues the project charter. According to the Project Management Institute's *PMBOK Guide* (2004), the project charter, either directly or by reference to other documents, addresses requirements that satisfy customer, sponsor, and other stakeholder needs and expectations, business needs at a high level, and project purpose or justification. The project charter documents the project manager and authority level and formalizes existence of the project. It summarizes milestones and schedule, stakeholder influences, participation of other organizations, constraints, business case justification, and the budget.

Skilled project sponsors are able to prepare a draft of a project charter and work together with the project manager to complete the document. Preparing a project charter takes time and effort, both well spent. Its power lies in defining what you know and what you do not know about the project.

## One-to-One Relationship Discussion

A major problem in some organizations is that functional managers feel threatened by the project manager because the project manager is closer to the power, both in doing the actual work and in relating to higher-ups in the organization. The project manager may be attending upper managers' meetings or talking to them directly to inform them about project status. This appears to bypass the chain of command.

Such issues can usually be resolved by dialogue. Talking together regularly is a good approach. Schedule regular one-on-one discussions (at least weekly) between the sponsor and the project manager to keep each informed of what is going on and to agree on relative priorities that affect the project. Set an expectation that each will keep the other informed. A unique relationship exists when the project manager has easy access to the sponsor at all times. Good rapport is a valuable commodity that contributes greatly to project success. It also allows the project manager to give feedback to the sponsor, and vice versa, about how well they are being served and where changes may be helpful.

# Criteria List

Not every executive makes a good project sponsor. A project sponsor needs specific characteristics, skills, and attitudes that may not be common among executives in certain organizations:

- They are decision makers.
- They are passionate.
- They know the business.
- They know the customer or industry.
- They have a vision of the future.
- They have worked at mainstream activities in the organization.
- They are influential.
- They are visible.
- They work well with people.
- They complement the project manager or others on the team.
- They are knowledgeable in areas where the project team is not.
- They ask for volunteers, knowing that this approach elicits greater commitment to the project than being assigned.

Are we talking about a visionary or a leader?

Successful sponsors are successful leaders who have a vision and then put forth the effort to attain that vision. It is important to start sponsoring the project with the end in mind. If you can clearly see where you are going, you can get there. You do not need to know every step, but vision makes the decisions along the way a lot easier. Good sponsors identify the project vision for the team and instill confidence that they know how to get there and will find the means to do so.

Sponsors need to be able to take charge of a situation and find a way forward. They need intuition (and an inclination to heed their intuition). That is primarily an inborn trait that is difficult to develop through training.

## Top Ten List

We met and shared a meeting of the minds with Lonnie Pacelli (2005), president of Leading on the Edge International, at the PMI Global Congress in Toronto, where he presented his "Top Ten Attributes of a Great Project Sponsor":

1. Clearly understand the problem to be solved.

   The organization is trying to stop the hemorrhaging of an existing problem.

   The organization is trying to improve on something that may already be working.

   The organization is trying to prevent a problem from occurring.

2. Ensure that the solution fixes the problem.

   The solution focuses on root causes, not symptoms.

   There are no "pork-barrel" solutions included in the core solution.

   The project sponsor can clearly envision and articulate how the organization would benefit by implementing the solution.

3. Know where "good enough" is.

   The project team doesn't waste organization resources by overengineering a solution.

   The project team doesn't oversimplify things thereby underallocating resources to fix the problem.

4. Build the right team to solve the problem.

   Appoint a strong project manager capable of driving the solution.

   Secure the right resources the project manager needs to get the job done.

   Ensure that resources aren't over- or underallocated to the project.

   Remove nonperformers or poor fits as necessary.

5. Hold the team accountable for results.

> Meet with the team on an appropriate regular basis for status updates.

> Ask the tough questions, particularly of poor performers.

> Keep the team focused on dates and deliverables.

6. Know the big issues and what is needed to resolve them.

> Understand the outstanding big issues facing the team.

> Know what is needed of the project sponsor to help resolve the issues.

> Hold the team accountable for timely resolution of issues.

7. Be the advocate, coach, influencer, and battering ram.

> Be a partner to the project manager by helping think through tough problems.

> Evangelize the project to peer executives and others in the organization.

8. Make the thoughtful, tough decisions.

> Don't drag your feet on making decisions.

> Don't be afraid to make a good business decision that may be unpopular.

> Be willing to make a good business decision that may mean personal loss in stature in the organization.

9. Ensure that the project finishes strong.

> Keep the team focused on delivering until the bottom of the ninth is over.

> Resist the urge to take on additional work at the last minute.

> Keep resources in place to ensure success.

10. Know when to pull the plug.

> Recognize when a project isn't going to deliver the results as originally expected.

> Know when higher-priority projects supplant the current project.

> Don't be afraid to cut losses and stop a failed project.

To sum up, project sponsors are a crucial component of any project and can either ensure its success or seal its doom. Sponsors need to be active, aware, engaged, available, and willing to help the project manager and project team deliver results to the organization. It's a risk that can be easily mitigated on any project and can absolutely make the difference between success and failure.

We could not agree more with Pacelli's tried-and-true techniques to help project sponsors be more effective at ensuring project success.

## Case Study

Let us share Michael O'Brochta's exemplary story of his efforts within the United States government to obtain sponsorship for a massive Professional Project Manager Certification (PPMC) program at the Central Intelligence Agency (CIA).

> As the manager of the PPMC program, I have recognized that since this effort broadly affects thousands of project managers, their advancement and assignments, and the culture in which they work, an unwavering commitment from executive sponsors is critical. This sponsorship support was achieved through a continuous process that began three years earlier when I listed the names of fifteen executives most likely to play a role in the sponsorship of this program. Working with a core member of my project team, I analyzed the role that each of these executives would need to play for the PPMC program to succeed. Some of the executive sponsors would need to contribute financial backing, others would need to exercise the authority associated with their official positions as chairpersons of the three project management occupations within the CIA, and still others would need to demonstrate support through highly visible participation in the program. Working first with the most supportive of these executive sponsors, I established relationships with each of them in descending order of their anticipated support, saving the least supportive for last.

For the executive sponsors likely to be the most supportive, the strategy employed to establish or reinforce their support was to focus on the organization benefit from the PPMC program and the long-lasting cultural legacy they would be contributing to; this approach appealed to their established ideology. For the executive sponsors who were likely to be the least supportive or resistant, the strategy used was to take advantage of the significant amount of support being provided by their peers to sway their attitudes. The methodology used to garner support from the project management occupation chairpersons was to highlight the fact that with little or no investment on their part, they could use PPMC as a tool or technique to quickly and effectively strengthen the occupations for which they were responsible. Financial sponsors were urged to contribute voluntarily as an alternative to having a tax imposed on their budgets by their already supportive superiors.

An approach used with all the executive sponsors was the consistent reminder from their own project manager employees about the value of the PPMC program. These employee efforts to garner sponsorship support for PPMC were coordinated and facilitated by a project management standards working group. I formed and led this voluntary community of practice by building on the fact that PPMC was a bottom-up type of program targeted at the needs of project managers and being led by project managers. I believe that the use of this working group to leverage the broad support from project managers throughout the CIA was the single biggest contributor to establishing and maintaining executive project sponsorship.

As a consultant for executives who have an interest in achieving a level of excellence in how they perform their roles as project sponsors, I have found that many of these executives simply do not know how to be effective sponsors. Some of them have had experience as project managers themselves and struggle to apply those skills in their roles as project sponsors. Others with backgrounds not in project management struggle too. As the PPMC program grows to serve the needs of more and more project managers within the CIA, a proportional increase in the number of executives are finding themselves in increasingly unfamiliar and sometimes uncomfortable situations as project sponsors. My advice to them has been direct and simply stated: "Behave like an executive sponsor." Sometimes the advice is focused on what not to do: "Stop behaving like a project manager." I inform them that an executive sponsor is in a support role; the purpose is to support the project manager. I encourage them to begin this support role by asking the single most powerful question a project sponsor can ask: "What can I do to help?" And I encourage them to maintain regular contact with the managers of the projects they are supporting and repeatedly to ask this same question. From that single question, several avenues of support frequently arise, including conflict resolution with competing customers and requirements, the prioritization of competing projects, and the freeing up of tight resources.

## Summary

This chapter covers various ways to go about the process of obtaining sponsors. The sponsor role may have different meanings, depending on the project management culture of the organization.

Sometimes project sponsors choose to be sponsors; sometimes they are assigned the role without being asked. The best project sponsors are those who understand their role and want to be in it.

Selling project sponsorship is a difficult task in many organizations. Normally, upper managers are responsible to look for the right project sponsor, and they follow their instincts. The fact is that not everyone can be a good sponsor; the role requires numerous special characteristics.

Obtaining a project sponsor takes time, and the organization needs to set out criteria to help in the selection process. Depending on the project management maturity level of the organization, this process will be effective or just remain another bureaucratic exercise. Apply reciprocity thinking to address both how the organization will benefit and what sponsors take away from their participation in the role.

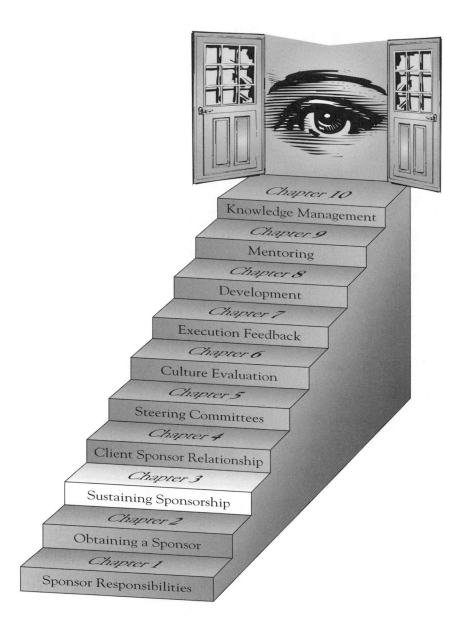

Chapter 10
Knowledge Management

Chapter 9
Mentoring

Chapter 8
Development

Chapter 7
Execution Feedback

Chapter 6
Culture Evaluation

Chapter 5
Steering Committees

Chapter 4
Client Sponsor Relationship

Chapter 3
Sustaining Sponsorship

Chapter 2
Obtaining a Sponsor

Chapter 1
Sponsor Responsibilities

# 3

# SUSTAINING SPONSORSHIP

He who loses wealth loses much; he who loses a friend
loses more; but he that loses his courage loses all.
— *Miguel de Cervantes*

A major problem with project sponsors is to keep them involved
and committed to the project during the complete project life cycle.
We often find that the sponsor of the delivery organization is very
committed from the beginning of the project until the sale is done,
at which point the sponsor disappears. One reason for this behavior is that project sponsors do not realize the need for continuous
project sponsorship all the way through to the end. Different per-
sonality styles, lack of knowledge, different priorities, and lack of interest are other reasons. The sponsor may not have been very
committed to the project in the first place or may be too busy with
other things. If sponsors are given sales objectives, they tend to
move on when sales are complete. Perhaps it did not occur to them
that by continuing as project sponsors and staying active, they
would know the customer much better and be able to sell more.
The measurement system may focus only on short-term, silo-based
activities and reward efficient individual efforts instead of optimizing organizational throughput and accomplishment. The sponsor
can bring perspective, reinforce the big picture, and fortify or di-
minish project effort based on strategic goals.

This chapter covers the challenges to sustaining excellence in
sponsorship throughout the project life cycle and the means you
may employ to communicate better.

## Challenges to Address

The activities to perform, as a project sponsor, vary during a project life cycle. The level of involvement is also different. Project sponsors are of more help to project managers and their teams when the sponsors provide support but do not interfere. During the initiation and planning phases, the sponsor plays an active role in helping establish project objectives. The sponsor guides the project manager to make decisions during the organization and staffing phases. The project sponsor is probably more familiar with organizational politics and can help navigate around the political factors that influence project execution.

A problem that often comes up is changes to project priorities. The project sponsor can work alone or with other executives to agree on project priority and then inform the project manager, explaining reasons why that priority was assigned. Project sponsors are managers or upper managers who know or should know how the organization works. Then the project sponsor can also help the project manager in establishing processes and procedures for the project. The project sponsor functions as the contact point for customers and clients. Customers and clients want to talk to people at the same level—the project manager from the project provider talks to the project manager for the customer, but the managing director wants to talk to another managing director.

Some delivery organizations in the solution business assign the project manager as the unique point of contact for everything, but that does not work well for upper-level people all the time.

How the sponsor supports project managers and operates within a working relationship makes a big difference in performance, experience, and learning. In a well-known multinational company, I (Bucero) tried to manage a project as a project manager, but my project sponsor (the top manager of the company) often interfered, not giving me the benefit of the doubt. Some hardware that needed to be delivered to our customer was delayed. I managed that situation by asking the sales organization to lend hardware temporarily to the customer. At the same time, my sponsor talked to the hardware division in Germany and got the equipment to the customer site in only three days. Sometimes I felt oversupported and sometimes the opposite. I felt undermined when the sponsor talked behind my back to the rest of the project team. However, on other occasions, he empowered me by talking in front of customer upper management, saying, "Alfonso is the right person. He is not alone. We as an organization and I personally will support him in case of issues or problems. You can have every confidence in Alfonso." . . . I felt confused. Later on, I understood that he was testing my capability for dealing with people; he put me into the circus in front of the lions to see what my reactions would be.

I was always persistent and dealt with the lions and received only minor scrapes and bruises. My learning outcome was great. Project managers can learn a lot from these situations, but they can also suffer when working under that kind of uncertainty. When project managers spend time talking to sponsors, they learn about the business context, company policies, and business restrictions. During the execution phase of a project, the sponsor has to be very careful when the project manager needs the sponsor to solve a problem. But if sponsors are too present during that phase, they can undermine the project manager's authority in front of team members. The confusing personal situation I just described occurred because the project sponsor relied solely on his intuition—he was not trained in or sensitive to being effective in his sponsor role.

We strongly recommend assigning one sponsor for the entire project. In long-term projects (ones that last more than two years), different project sponsors can be assigned for different phases. One criterion for who should be the sponsor is identifying who has a vested interest in or special skills for that stage of the project.

## Proactive Sponsorship

The ideal situation is proactive sponsorship—getting a project sponsor who is committed, accountable, serious about the project, knowledgeable, trained, and able not only to talk the talk but also to walk the walk. Such people are trustworthy in all respects. Their values are transparent and aligned with the organization and its strategy. Such sponsors protect the team from disruptive outside influences and back the team up when times are tough. It is far better to start out with the right sponsor than having to correct a bad sponsorship situation down the road. That is why it is so important to select the right sponsor and train the person for the role, as discussed in many of the chapters in this book. An organizational culture committed to this approach is a desired goal. It represents a well-developed, mature organization.

If  your eyes are rolling and you are wondering if we are living in a dream world, please do not blame us for trying. We would be remiss if we did not say do it right the first time and save yourself grief later on. The best way to sustain good sponsorship is to start out with good sponsorship. Anything less is remedial.

How do you set up such a world? Put the time and effort into selling the concept of sponsorship excellence. This works especially well during a revitalization model when coming out of the cultural distortion stage and a new leader comes into the organization (see Graham and Englund, 2004, ch. 1). Be first in line to get everyone's attention and commitment. Include a coalition of supporters that brings a critical mass to this effort. Ask and answer questions about the potential to accomplish more when excellent project sponsorship is the routine way of doing business. Describe the benefits of improved performance, productive experiences, and competitive advantage based on accelerated learning. Point out the negative consequences when projects lack upper management support. Describe a desired state where more is possible because upper managers work together across the organization to pick the right projects and do the projects right. Advance a plan for sponsorship training, networking opportunities for sponsors, and clear roles and responsibilities. Establish and expect accountable work practices whereby all participants accept accountability for the success of an organic organization—a project-based organization structured naturally to solve problems—not just operating with a narrow focus on their small piece within the project or organization. Know that a worthy effort was put into creating a proactive sponsorship culture. Start now because it takes a while (a long while!) to change a culture that may be lacking.

## Project Reviews

To create a good relationship between the project manager and the project sponsor takes time and needs fine tuning. One method we have found useful and strongly recommend is to run monthly project reviews led by the project sponsor. Those meetings add value to the project manager, to the project sponsor, and to the organization. They force the project manager to review his or her project status and pending tasks. At the same time, they force the project sponsor to know more about the project, the customer, and other project stakeholders. In the solution business, for example, that practice helps the project sponsor know the customer much better and therefore generate more business.

One approach to project reviews is to have them organized by the project management office (PMO). This has helped us discover a number of key issues where lack of knowledge was present and bad practices were being employed. Such discussions usually happen on troubled projects, but when business results are on target, management teams do not give enough priority to these issues.

Doing those reviews, sponsors will be better prepared to react on the basis of fresh information. If sponsors are involved sooner in the project life cycle, making decisions is easier. What you know about the project and what you don't know about the project are fundamental determinants of project success. Figure 3.1 depicts the level of knowledge you have on a project as time goes on. At the beginning, ordinarily, you have very little knowledge about the project, and at the end, you have full project knowledge. That means you usually have a lot of uncertainty along the project life cycle. That level of uncertainty needs to be diminished—but how to do it? Ask questions of all project stakeholders. A sponsor's efficacy may be known by the quality of questions asked. Many questions are more valuable than their answers because they cause people to think and act differently. Many questions do not have easy answers, but questions about

## Figure 3.1  The Knowledge Curve

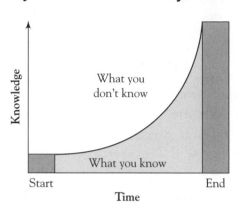

project status need answering by the project manager and other project stakeholders. If the sponsor does not get answers to these questions, he or she will nevertheless take some kind of immediate action, and that action may not be in the best interest of the project.

A global project review process may consist of various types of reviews, depending on project stage. There are four typical review types:

- Initiation review (IR)
- Planning and proposal review (PPR)
- Procurement review (PR)
- Quality assurance review (QAR)

A good way to start the review process is to examine ongoing projects, looking for deviations and variations. This information can then be presented on a regular basis to the management team. This helps sponsors see the reasons for project variances and deviations and also the reasons behind recommendations for the new action plan.

Project success depends on the ability to translate knowledge into added value for customers as a result of the project life cycle. Although projects are unique, the experiences learned on each project can be applied in similar projects. To do so, it is necessary to establish and implement internal processes to be followed by project teams after projects are completed.

The process of capturing team experiences and examining variances and deviations from the project plan helps increase productivity and improve organizational success. There are several objectives for these project reviews:

- Determining the feasibility of the project and helping the management team make go or no-go decisions, based on review results
- Checking if all necessary activities were done before presenting a customer proposal or solution
- Checking if all formal agreements and procedures were formally accepted and reviewed between the customer and the project delivery organization
- Tracking deviations and variances and allowing room for improvements and action plans

## When to Do Project Reviews

When should you do a project review? Whenever you can learn something that will contribute to performance improvement. When starting a sponsorship initiative, we initially decided to do a review after each project milestone. Depending on the size and complexity of the project, monthly reviews are generally adequate. The content of each review may be the same, but due to variations in project type, they may be longer or shorter. Figure 3.2 depicts a life cycle chart that includes a review at each major milestone.

**Figure 3.2 Project Life Cycle with Scheduled Project Reviews**

Bearing in mind the main objectives of extracting benefit from experiences, learning from failures, and preparing action plans when necessary, time and effort for this activity will happen when it is expected, authorized, and supported by the project sponsor. Keeping projects on track is one of the main responsibilities of the project manager. Reviews are proactive actions that allow the project manager to analyze the project status in a formal way, communicate with the sponsor, and jointly take necessary actions in case of variances or deviations. Regular reviews and taking actions on findings improve an organization's maturity in project management. They therefore need to be approved and supported by all upper-level managers in the organization.

## How to Do Project Reviews

Reviews are best conducted face to face, although in some situations and due to geographical diversity, other approaches, such as telephone conferences or videoconferences, may be necessary. Reducing the cost of these sessions is very important, particularly on big or multisite projects in a slow economy.

Face-to-face sessions generally should not exceed two hours. Be aware, however, that if they are being conducted by phone, it is difficult to keep the attention of participants for more than about an hour. Detailed preparation for these reviews is essential for success, forcing the project manager to stop daily management activity and think about project status. The effort of thinking about the project and analyzing all the facts and data is worthwhile.

The PMO can facilitate these reviews by using a checklist and providing a PM expert to conduct them. Having people external to the project facilitate the review is good because they can analyze project status more objectively.

Conduct quality assurance reviews throughout project execution. QARs can provide an overview like the one in Figure 3.3, which shows status in different colors to indicate results of assessments in every knowledge area.

Produce this overview as an output of the review. In our example, we used experienced project managers as reviewers. The

## Figure 3.3  Quality Assurance Review Process Chart

| | |
|---|---|
| Organization: | ESD |
| Client: | XYZW |
| Project Name: | Example |
| Project ID: | 99IF0001 |

| | |
|---|---|
| Proj. Mgr/Dir.: | Randy Gil |
| Tech. Mgr/Lead: | FSI |
| Department Manager: | D. Walls |

| | |
|---|---|
| Business Reviewer: | Susan Holiday |
| Financial Reviewer: | Bob Martinez |
| Review Date: | 24-abr-01 |

**Overall Project Assessment:** | Green |

| Area | Included* | Assessment |
|---|---|---|
| Scope | Yes | Yellow |
| Time | Yes | Red |
| Cost/Rev. | Yes | Red |
| Quality | Yes | Yellow |
| Resource | Yes | Green |
| Communication | Yes | Green |
| Risk | Yes | Green |
| Contracts | Yes | Green |
| Client Satisfaction | Yes | Red |

**Overall Assessment Key:**

| | |
|---|---|
| Red | Critical or significant issues or major process noncompliance |
| Yellow | Unless immediate action is taken, project may become red |
| Green | No significant nonconformance foreseeable at this time |

### Scoring Guidelines:

| | |
|---|---|
| 0 | Nothing done, no results, no process in place or No to Yes/No question |
| 1 | Work started in this area, but major improvement required |
| 2 | Some work done in this area, some results achieved, but needs some improvement |
| 3 | Meets requirements and expectations, no significant problems, or Yes for Y/N question |
| 4 | Above average results and process in place, well managed and executed |
| 5 | Exceptional results, "best in class" referenceable material |

*Note: Where the answer to a Yes/No question is Yes, present it, or its results, for the reviewer.

## Figure 3.3  Quality Assurance Review Process Chart, Cont'd.

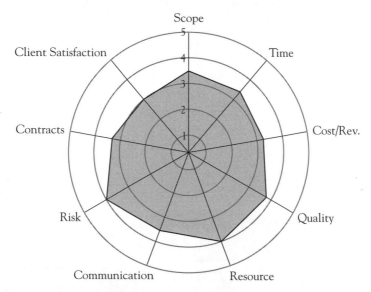

Project Quality Assessment

indicators of this view relate to PMBOK areas and actual status. Based on those results, the project sponsor and the project manager agreed on an action plan, which they would revisit in the next project review. Each project manager would be interviewed by the reviewer, who was guided by his PM experience, common sense, and a checklist with questions following the main areas in the body of knowledge (see Figure 3.4). Using these tools vastly increases the extent and quality of communications with the project sponsor.

## Review Questionnaire

One of the project sponsor's roles is to verify not only that the project manager is managing the project properly but also that the manager is doing the right tasks that contribute to project and organization success.

Figure 3.5 may be used by the project sponsor as a questionnaire or reminder that key elements of proactive sponsorship are being considered and executed.

# Figure 3.4  Questions Asked by the Reviewer

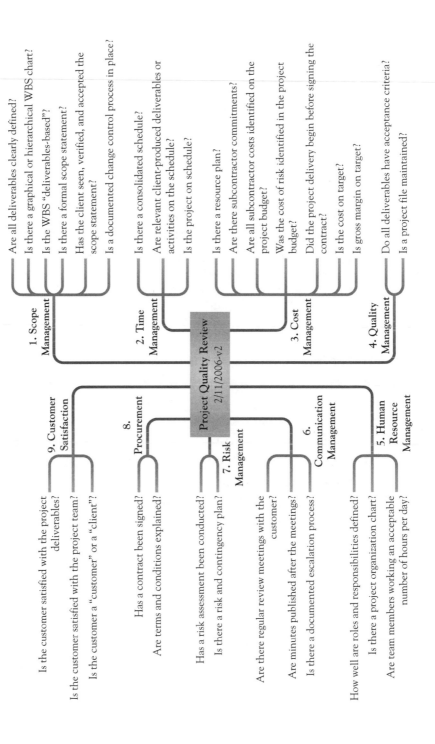

**Project Quality Review**
2/11/2006-v2

**1. Scope Management**
- Are all deliverables clearly defined?
- Is there a graphical or hierarchical WBS chart?
- Is the WBS "deliverables-based"?
- Is there a formal scope statement?
- Has the client seen, verified, and accepted the scope statement?
- Is a documented change control process in place?

**2. Time Management**
- Is there a consolidated schedule?
- Are relevant client-produced deliverables or activities on the schedule?
- Is the project on schedule?

**3. Cost Management**
- Is there a resource plan?
- Are there subcontractor commitments?
- Are all subcontractor costs identified on the project budget?
- Was the cost of risk identified in the project budget?
- Did the project delivery begin before signing the contract?
- Is the cost on target?
- Is gross margin on target?

**4. Quality Management**
- Do all deliverables have acceptance criteria?
- Is a project file maintained?

**9. Customer Satisfaction**
- Is the customer satisfied with the project deliverables?
- Is the customer satisfied with the project team?
- Is the customer a "customer" or a "client"?

**8. Procurement**
- Has a contract been signed?
- Are terms and conditions explained?

**7. Risk Management**
- Has a risk assessment been conducted?
- Is there a risk and contingency plan?

**6. Communication Management**
- Are there regular review meetings with the customer?
- Are minutes published after the meetings?
- Is there a documented escalation process?

**5. Human Resource Management**
- How well are roles and responsibilities defined?
- Is there a project organization chart?
- Are team members working an acceptable number of hours per day?

### Figure 3.5  A Questionnaire for Proactive Sponsorship

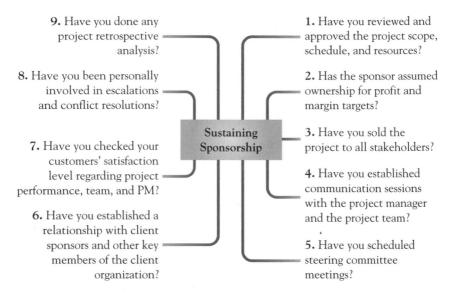

9. Have you done any project retrospective analysis?

8. Have you been personally involved in escalations and conflict resolutions?

7. Have you checked your customers' satisfaction level regarding project performance, team, and PM?

6. Have you established a relationship with client sponsors and other key members of the client organization?

Sustaining Sponsorship

1. Have you reviewed and approved the project scope, schedule, and resources?

2. Has the sponsor assumed ownership for profit and margin targets?

3. Have you sold the project to all stakeholders?

4. Have you established communication sessions with the project manager and the project team?

5. Have you scheduled steering committee meetings?

1.  The interactions between project sponsor and project manager are definitive for project success. The project manager is mired in daily project work and sometimes cannot see the whole picture. The project sponsor helps keep perspective. To do that, a good level of communication must exist. The project manager and customer can define project scope, but the project sponsor ensures that all parties formally agree on the project scope. The same applies for schedule and resources. Not verifying project expectations is one prominent reason for project failure.

2.  In the solution business, every project is measured by target profit and margin. The project manager needs to put in the work to make results happen and to share accountability for project outcome financials. However, ownership for achieving benefits or return on investment after the work is done and throughout the project *outcome* life cycle resides primarily with the project sponsor. Linking the project to strategic goals, setting objectives, implementing a balanced scorecard, and making decisions consistent with these goals and objectives are steps for which the sponsor

needs to take ownership. Plan to actively follow through after project deliverables have been produced to ensure that the end user or customer gets value and that expected benefits occur. Unfortunately, many projects produce "stuff" that just goes "on the shelf," never to see the light of day again. The sponsor closes the loop to ensure that project outcomes are productive or modified to be useful and that the organization only completes projects that are truly necessary.

3. The project sponsor needs to be a good salesperson, convincing other stakeholders about the benefits of doing the project. Constantly develop and apply selling skills. Make the effort to identify and then describe the features, benefits, and advantages that specific stakeholders care about, using vivid language and convincing data. Success requires believing in the project; a person who does not believe in something is not able to sell it to other people.

4. A good project manager spends 90 percent of his or her time communicating. The project sponsor also needs to be a good communicator. The sponsor may run some meetings with the project manager and team members, not only when problems arise but systematically during the project life cycle. This active presence demonstrates a commitment level that contributes to improved team morale.

5. Project sponsors have a responsibility to update senior managers with project status information. They also need periodically to validate project scope with organizational goals that may change. Because of that, schedule and organize regular steering committee meetings. Use these steering committees as a means for upper managers to work together as a team. Demonstrate desired teamwork behaviors that set the pace for the rest of the organization: engage in constructive conflict, discuss and agree on strategic goals, establish consistent criteria for prioritizing projects and resource allocation, and follow through on decisions made.

6. The more the project sponsor knows about the project and its environment, the smaller the risk of failure. Help and support

the project manager in any area where he or she may not possess the knowledge or experience to solve a problem, especially in areas outside the project's immediate work environment. Be available and approachable. Create a relationship with the customer and other members of the organization. Develop a reputation as trustworthy, because the trust factor, when lacking, can seriously undermine cooperation, perhaps more than any other single factor. People need to know each other well in order to do business together. It is easier to solve problems when the project sponsor knows the requirements or needs from the customer.

7. The main purpose of most projects is to achieve mission and project objectives according to customer requirements. The project sponsor needs to verify in every steering committee meeting that stakeholder expectations are being met. Also check periodically on customer satisfaction levels regarding the project team and project manager performance. Surface any issues early, and be prepared to take action in the event of customer dissatisfaction.

8. Issues or problems arise on every project and ordinarily, the project manager and team cannot resolve them all. The project sponsor, as coach, mentor, and ultimate decision maker, is a ready resource for the team to draw on when the going gets tough. Early in the project, establish an escalation process, including triggers and criteria, for issues that will need the sponsor's attention. If no problems have been escalated to the sponsor for a long time, a wise move is to verify that everything is okay. Sometimes the level of communication between sponsor and project manager is inadequate or not working properly. In that case, have a meeting with the project manager and clarify the situation.

9. Retrospective analysis is beneficial for all project stakeholders and the prosperity of the organization. The project sponsor is the right person to instigate these sessions during the project life cycle. Spend time discussing what you learn, what was good and not good, and what to repeat, continue doing, or stop doing. All learning involves movement between reflection and action. Teams notice

when sponsors listen, apply their acquired judgment, and take responsible action.

Reviews are among the best practices that sponsors can conduct with their project managers. The lesson learned when they start to know their customers, their needs, and the project management discipline can lead to substantial increases in profitable business. This increased involvement means that project sponsorship is sustained from project initiation through to the end. Managers see how excellence in project sponsorship contributes added value both personally and organizationally.

Careful measures provide early warnings and lead to more options for corrective actions. Project reviews provide proactive status reports to avoid surprises and escalate problems or issues detected when appropriate. They are also a vehicle for learning how to improve the project management process.

## Moving Forward Through Sponsorship

Lessons learned from past projects provide lots of evidence for the importance of good sponsorship. More often than not, at the heart of failed projects, the underlying reason is poor sponsorship.

The most important thing sponsors can do is recognize their role and exercise the traits of good sponsorship. Daryl Conner (1993) of ODR Inc. identifies six characteristics of strong sponsorship (see Table 3.1). Interestingly, many of these traits could be attributed to leadership, such as vision, sense of urgency, and public and private modeling. The main trait that clearly distinguishes sponsors is their power and authority to legitimize the change. Unlike other leaders, sponsors hold the pursestrings and possess legitimacy and authority to do whatever is necessary to enable the achievement of transformation objectives. Also, sponsors, because of their power and position, have leverage, or the ability to use consequences, both positive and negative, to reinforce desired new behaviors.

#### Table 3.1  The Six Characteristics of Strong Sponsorship

| Characteristic | Definition | Sponsor Actions |
|---|---|---|
| Power | The authority to legitimize the project within the organization | Acquires and deploys the necessary resources |
| Sense of urgency | The compelling project need to transform elements of the business system in a timely manner | Overcomes all obstacles to achieve the desired state |
| Vision | A clear, tangible, and accessible description of the desired state | Creates an active dialogue about the desired state with all constituencies |
| Public role | Public communication and reinforcement of all aspects of the transformation | Discusses and reinforces the need to achieve the desired state during public and visible day-to-day activities |
| Private role | Private communication and reinforcement of all aspects of the project | Meets with key individuals to discuss the need for the project and reinforces the role that each individual must play |
| Leverage | Use of consequences, both rewards and punishments, to reinforce the new behaviors associated with the desired state | Rewards (or punishes) individuals and constituencies throughout the project process for behavior or activity that is consistent (or inconsistent) with the desired state, as appropriate |

## Sponsorship in New Product Development

Paul O'Connor (2006) of The Adept Group Limited, Inc. (www.adept-plm.com) offers a simple formula that applies to achieving excellence in project sponsorship when applied to new product development (NPD).

Improvement in NPD output cannot come from increased work effort by individuals. People are simply tapped-out on how much time they can give and how hard they can work. While NPD professionals used to live by the mantra "do more with less," we now seem to be shifting our mantra to "do lots more with a little bit more."

Alignment, integration, and facilitation are requisite to improved NPD proficiency when the organization is already running lean. To gain it, most organizations will have to revamp the way they work, communicate, and make decisions. The formula for doing so, though, is straightforward. First, spot an accomplished and influential NPD executive [project sponsor] willing to get into the NPD trenches. Next, help this key executive understand that improvement lies with the work processes and methods of the organization as a whole, not by demanding more of individuals. Then add to the mix a deep understanding of seven components of improvement. This potent combination will deliver increased NPD output even when the organization is running lean:

1. Rationalize your organization's mix of NPD projects.

2. Revamp your NPD processes and facilitate them with software to:

    • Shorten and speed up the stage-gate process;

    • Establish a defined and highly proactive front-end process;

    • Precede all NPD work with intelligent and methodical product line planning (including technology mapping and market mapping).

3. Invest in meaningful Voice of the Customer training and facilitation/support tools to drive and influence concept generation during the front-end process.

4. Establish and adhere to sound project management and portfolio management practices.

5. Integrate information, data, and all bits of knowledge across all NPD processes and with the core business.

6. Analyze and then align the full decision-flow and the full workflow of your NPD efforts (from pre-concept to post launch and product retirement).

7. Enable modeling of specific elements of risk for each project and for the full portfolio of projects.

## My Role as Program Sponsor, by Michael O'Brochta

As manager of the Professional Project Manager Program (PPMC) at the CIA, I understood that my role involved wearing multiple hats. While my primary duties were associated with my positional authority as program manager, I also served in the role of program sponsor. In this regard, I looked for ways to support key members of the program team as well as key stakeholders in the program. This sponsor support that I performed took several forms and was not unlike what is described by Robert Greenleaf in his book *Servant Leadership* (1977).

For me, providing support to others was the most important aspect of being a sponsor. This support was targeted at creating an environment so they could make the most significant contribution they were capable of making to the program—an environment where they could excel. Given the diversity associated with the program members and stakeholders, communication ended up being the key to providing this support. This diversity occurred because of the mix of multiple contractors involved in the program, the mix of skill sets involved in the program, the geographical separation between those involved in the program, the fact that the majority of those in the program had not worked together before, and the highly divergent backgrounds of those involved in the program. I invested my time and resources heavily in writing down enough about the program so that this diverse cast of characters could perform as effectively and efficiently as possible. Standards and procedures were written and shared. Reviews and technical exchange meetings were held on a continuous basis. Announcements and Web site postings were frequently released.

In response to this sponsor communications support, I expected the program members and stakeholders to become reliant on this information, and I expected them *not* to rely on other sources of competing and conflicting information. I expected that they would treat this information as the single authoritative source. I expected that if we adopted a standard for content or a standard for administration, all would be familiar with the standard, all would use it, and all would hold one another accountable for using it. I also expected that when this information was found to be lacking in some way, they would take the initiative to improve it. As part of this sponsor communications support, I provided a standard mechanism for managing change. I expected that when an initiative was taken to improve on some of the information provided, this standard mechanism for managing change would be used.

My role as program sponsor was influenced by the authority and latitude given to me by my boss. I was given as much as I needed and wanted; more was not necessary. His visible demonstrations of deference to my authority strengthened my ability to serve as program manager and program sponsor.

## Summary

Leaders become better prepared as sponsors of major projects by taking inventory of their talents and skills and putting appropriate action plans in place. Success starts with a strong commitment to improve. Set a goal of proactive sponsorship. However, perfection in sponsoring a project is almost impossible, but taking the journey to become more effective sponsors, fully aware and ready for action, is worth the effort.

As in other endeavors involving multitasking, if you chase two rabbits, you lose them both. Share of mind and sponsorship attention can make or break project success. Since adequate management attention is one of the scarcest resources, focusing on fewer projects at a time and limiting the number of projects that a manager sponsors makes excellence in project sponsorship more achievable.

Assess the challenges that inhibit a sustainable sponsorship culture. Gather the knowledge, and with help from your colleagues, begin the change process that taps the unique power and position held by sponsors. Establish regular communications between sponsors and project managers. Conduct project reviews, and act on emergent lessons. Enforce commitments. Above everything else, practice accountability at all levels of the organization for optimizing a level of proficiency that can best be achieved through collaboration on project-based work.

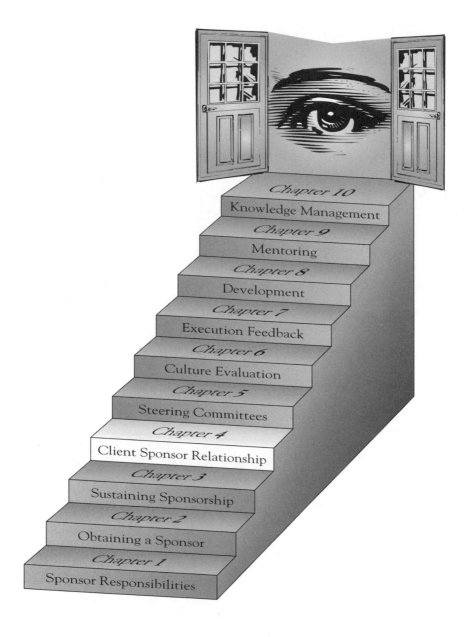

# 4

# CLIENT SPONSOR RELATIONSHIP

Destiny is no matter of chance. It is a matter of
choice. It is not a thing to be waited for; it is a
thing to be achieved.

—*William Jennings Bryan*

Clients expect value added from service providers. Providers need
to be seen as leaders in front of customers. You have to know the
value systems of the executives in the client organization if you
want to impress them. A wise approach is always to "seek first to
understand." Find out what their goals are. Find out their communication style. Find out what issues or problems they are dealing
with, and help them find solutions.

Sometimes you can help executives get promoted, and this situation makes room for you to move forward. Let them know you
need their help along the project life cycle. Help client sponsors get
what they want and help them look good to their bosses, and reap
the benefits of repeat business. Help others, and they will keep you
around as they move forward.

Taking into account that client expectations will change because clients are, after all, human beings, how can you discover what
they want? At any given moment, they probably know what they
*know* and what they *don't know* about their project requirements.

This chapter covers the special situation when providers do
work for clients. The terms *customer* and *client* are used almost
interchangeably. Client relationships tend to be more intensive
because clients usually request that a project be done for them,

whereas customers may simply purchase the outcome from the project. We describe ways to improve relationships between provider sponsors and client sponsors by focusing on communication. We also provide general advice on gaining credibility that is applicable to all relationships. The point is to put extra effort into creating and maintaining the relationship.

## Creating and Maintaining the Relationship

When a project starts, one question that comes to mind is, What does the client want from us as professionals and as an organization? In other words, what does the client expect from us as a result of the project?

The role played by project sponsors in customer relations depends on the type of client and organization. Usually, clients want to be informed regularly about project status. They want an open path of communication between sponsors. Speaking the truth from project initiation on is one key for project success. The provider sponsor and the client sponsor need to be open and transparent, creating the right environment for project success. A relationship with a client is a process of human interaction but also a work in progress. It involves much more than just an exchange of money and services.

Most client relationships are based on conversations. The project sponsor starts the client relationship through conversations so that he or she can make the necessary management decisions and take appropriate actions during the project life cycle. Creating and maintaining that relationship requires special skills in information gathering, talking, and follow-up (see Figure 4.1).

### Figure 4.1  Special Skills for Relationships

| Gathering | Talking | Follow-Up |
|---|---|---|
| • Focuses on the customer | • Focuses on the relationship | • Focuses on management decisions |
| • Understanding customer needs | • Conversation | |
| | • Added value | |

*Information gathering* focuses on the customer. It is intended to help learn more about the client, the environment, and behavior patterns or customer reactions during the project life cycle. Understanding what is urgent from the client's perspective is the basis for recognizing and understanding customer needs.

*Talking* focuses on the relationship. It is intended to ensure that value is created in every conversation with the client. The client expects to get some value from the provider because that is what the client is paying for. The provider needs to be proactive in dealing with facts, anticipating needs, and taking advantage of prior experiences and knowledge.

*Follow-up* focuses on management decisions that need to be made concerning organizational and management mechanisms that enable continued information gathering and talking. Provider and client sponsors need to meet periodically on their own, not just in project steering committee meetings.

Information gathering, talking, and follow-up are not just a "to do" list for sponsors. They are not a sequence of tasks or steps. Rather, they are separate sponsor-focused, day-to-day preoccupations that create good sponsor relationships.

Following are some suggested questions for information gathering, talking and follow-up. (See also Figure 4.2.)

### Information Gathering

Who is my customer? The customer's customer?

What are the client's personal and professional expectations?

What is our value as perceived by the client?

### Talking

What type of relationship do I want to build with my client?

How do we foster exchange?

How do we work together and share control?

What unique control mechanism ensures we are on track?

### Figure 4.2  Questions to Guide the Client Sponsor Relationship

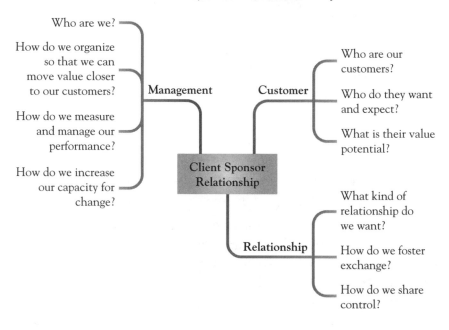

*Follow-Up*

Who are we?

How do I organize to move value closer to the client?

How do we measure and manage our performance?

How do we increase our capacity for change?

By asking these types of questions, project sponsors will be able to guide the evolution of relationships with their clients.

On one project I (Bucero) managed, the client was unhappy with the attitude and actions of the assigned project sponsor. The project was two and a half years long and involved about 150 people on the project team. The project sponsor from the service provider attended all the steering committee meetings every month and actively participated during the preliminary sales phase. But he was not actively involved in contract negotiations, and he visited the client only once a month, on the day of the steering committee meeting. Sometimes I felt he delegated too many things to me as project manager. It was very difficult for him to understand the pressure I suffered during the project life cycle because he was not living on the client site every day.

Many times I needed to make a decision because I did not have access to my sponsor (provider sponsor). I was not the right person to make some decisions, but I had to do it. The client recognized that the project lacked adequate sponsorship from the provider, but he also recognized my effort as a project manager to move the project forward. Ramifications of that recognition were that I was invited to the Client Executive Committee to report on project status. The client wanted me attending that meeting instead of my sponsor. Little by little, I gained customer credibility. At the end of the project, the client sent a complaining letter saying that the project had no provider sponsor but the project manager was able to work very successfully with the provider project manager.

## Client Expectations

These are some things clients expect from project sponsors (as solution providers):

- Clients want active participation during the preliminary sales phase and contract negotiation and also during the rest of the project life cycle. The project manager should not be the only person at the customer site dealing with client management. The client sponsor must deal with the provider sponsor.

- They expect to establish and maintain a high-level client relationship. That means that the solution provider sponsor talks to the client sponsor frequently, and they deal with project strategy and issues together. The most important considerations are always what is best for project success.

- They expect the sponsor to assist the project manager in getting the project under way (planning, staffing, and so forth). Clients sense when the provider project manager feels alone or unsupported. Adequate levels of support demonstrate the maturity level or measure of advancement in project management discipline implementation of the provider organization.

- They want to know current information regarding main activities of the project. Information can be shared by phone, but we recommend that the project sponsor and project manager have a weekly meeting to keep both updated—twenty to thirty minutes may be enough, depending on the type of project.

- All contractual matters usually have legal implications and may involve strategic decisions in areas in which the project sponsor needs to be involved. Sharing contractual agreements between client and provider is fundamental and key for project success but also takes a lot of time. Lawyers are essential and very helpful in this matter.

- Company policies need to be conveyed by the project sponsor to project managers. Project sponsors are usually located at strategic levels in the organization and are more familiar with company policies.

- Clients expect provider sponsors to help project managers solve problems in which a business or strategic decision has to be made. The client pays the provider to add value.

- They want general managers and client managers to be kept advised about critical or significant project problems or issues. Because of the importance of these areas to a successful outcome, the relationship between the project sponsor and the project manager needs to be fluent and concise.

## Sustaining Supplier-Client Relationships

The project sponsor has the responsibility of maintaining executive customer contact. Doing this with excellence requires knowing the client sponsor extremely well, being open and transparent, and being able to establish a good relationship. The basis of a good relationship is truth. The win-win approach has more benefits than disadvantages for project success.

In addition to a sponsor, an assigned executive from senior management can be helpful. This person's role may be ceremonial at times but involves an ongoing commitment from the supplier to the client. The executive knows his or her counterparts in the other organization and is familiar with the history of the relationship. This executive meets with the client during company visits, expresses the highest level of support from the company, and can be called on if an issue needs escalation to the top of the company. An assigned executive represents a known person. Invoking this practice conveys that the company cares deeply about its best clients and accords them preferential treatment. It may also be the competitive advantage that allows the relationship to move forward.

Establishing good relationships between client and provider sponsor requires time together. They must talk with each other. In Spain, for instance, it is common to take a long lunch during which they get to know more about everyone's professional and personal objectives in a open environment. Professional relationships are human relationships; project sponsors also have personal and professional objectives for a particular project. The client wants to have a provider who is always available.

At the beginning of a project, the project sponsor is actively involved. For instance, he or she helps validate and set the project mission, objectives, and main priorities and responsibilities during the project start-up meeting. Upper managers and senior executives who act as project sponsors must establish project priorities for the projects for which they are assigned. However, in the execution phase, sponsors play a more reactive role; they act when requested by the project manager or by the client organization.

But project sponsors need to be careful that they are not involved in all project problems because that situation may undermine the authority of the project manager. Only the problem or issues that need business or strategic support or decisions should be solved by the project sponsor.

Key traits that enable a relationship to be sustained include trust in each other, confidence that the other has the skills and wherewithal to accomplish his or her commitments, and openness about all things good, bad, and ugly. The relationship needs to be perceived as a collaboration rather than a competition. It may also require that the parties sign a nondisclosure agreement to ensure that competitive information does not leak out.

When problems arise that do not appear solvable by the project team or linger beyond reasonable expectations, have a clearly defined escalation path or flowchart. Having this process mapped out before it is needed indicates a powerful commitment to satisfying the client. Likewise, the client sponsor may need to be called on when unreasonable demands or work outside the contract come up.

## Relationship Template

Table 4.1 provides a template for recording the outcome from the information-gathering, talking, and follow-up process, showing what is important for each sponsor. Documenting this information provides an overview of client sponsors and their agendas and knowledge level about the projects they sponsor. Use it to plan strategies for building and sustaining the relationships.

**Table 4.1  A Template for Client Sponsor Relationships**

| Client Sponsor (Name and Position) | Business Agenda for the Project | Personal Agenda | Project Knowledge Level | Relationship-Building Strategies |
|---|---|---|---|---|
|  |  |  |  |  |

## Gaining Credibility

People need time to build good relationships. Credibility is normally the result of applying authenticity and integrity in a relationship. Sometimes the provider sponsor concentrates on taking care of the project budget and forgets to focus on other aspects, including what is best for project success. At other times, the client sponsor tries to take advantage by setting up a win-lose relationship. That situation is also bad for project success.

In our opinion, credibility requires being able to establish a trust relationship in which the outcome is always win-win. Client sponsor credibility is like a building—it must be built brick by brick, and the mortar needs time to dry before building higher.

Not many organizations have a formal project management selection process in place. But all companies want to have the best project managers ready for managing projects successfully. Managers expect good project results, and team members want to have the best project managers to manage successful projects—good leaders that they will follow. Then the project manager must cultivate not only hard but also soft skills to be successful. Most soft skills are linked to people's attitudes and behaviors.

Organizations need project managers who are honest and competent and can also inspire people. For example, I (Bucero) was involved in a project whose objective was to move one organization from functional to project-oriented organization. I encountered a lot of resistance in the client organization and only a few believers. I tried to act honestly with everyone, and in many meetings, I said, "This change is difficult but not impossible." My principle is always that today is a good day. Everything can be changed in the project environment. I applied a disciplined process and always did what I promised I would do. I agreed with my client to present a project status report every Friday at 10:00 A.M., and I did. I planned to meet somebody at a determined date, and I did. Credibility is built through a succession of little details that accumulate over the course of a project. All must learn from the results and refine subsequent actions. That gives credibility. Credibility has to do with reputation.

Credibility is something that is earned over time. It does not come automatically with the job or the title. It begins early in our lives and careers.

A credibility foundation is built step by step during a professional career path. And as each step is achieved, the foundation of the future is gradually built. Team members do not want to follow a manager who is not credible, who does not truly believe in what he or she is doing and how he or she is doing it.

A manager's credibility has a significant positive outcome on individual and organizational performance. Real leaders strengthen the people around them and make others feel more important. Leaders also act as facilitators. The most important thing is the project, not the project sponsor or the project manager. Credibility can be defined as the behavioral evidence the participants would use to judge whether or not the project leader was believable. People commonly report that such leaders "do what they say they will do," "practice what they preach," or "walk the walk and talk the talk" (see Englund, 2000).

Credibility is mostly about consistency between words and deeds. Project stakeholders listen to the words and look at the deeds. Executive sponsors are expected to do what they say. They are expected to keep their promises and follow through on their commitments. But what they say must also be what team members believe. To take people to places they have never been before (as in achieving project results), project leaders and team need to be on the same path. And to get people to join the voyage of discovery voluntarily requires that the aims and aspirations of leaders and teams be harmonious.

Thinking "I" instead of "we" has generated many problems for project managers and executives. Their actions run the risk of being perceived as consistent only with their own wishes, not with those of the people they are supposed to lead. When managers resort to the use of power and position, to compliance and command to get things done, they are not leading; they are dictating.

The credible leader learns how to discover and communicate the shared values and visions that can form a common ground on which all can stand. Credible leaders find harmony among the diverse interests, points of view, and beliefs. Standing on a strong, unified foundation, project leaders and teams can act consistently with spirit and drive to build viable projects.

Three closely linked aspects combine to boost credibility: sharpness, harmony, and passion.

Commitment to credibility begins with *sharpness:* clarifying the leader's commitment, needs interests, values, visions, and project objectives.

To build a powerful and viable project, a project team needs to be in *harmony* about a common cause, united on where the team is going, why it is headed in that direction, and which principles will guide its actions.

Credible leaders need the ability to build a shared vision and values. Harmony exists when team members widely share, support, and endorse the intent of the commonly understood set of aims and aspirations. Not only do team members know what these are, but they are also in agreement that the shared vision and values are important to the future success of the project and the organization. They have a common interpretation of how the values will be put into practice.

Understanding and agreeing to aims and aspirations are essential to the process of strengthening credibility. But actions speak louder than words, so people who feel strongly about the worth of values will act on them. *Passion* is evident when principles are taken seriously; when they reflect deep feelings, standards, and emotional bonds; and when they are the basis of critical organizational resource allocations. When values are intensely felt, there is greater consistency between words and actions, and there is an almost moral dimension to "keeping the faith."

Sharpness, harmony, and passion provide a useful framework for looking at the process of strengthening credibility. But what about daily project manager actions? When asking project leaders across Europe to provide specific examples of what their most admired leaders do to gain respect, trust, and a willingness to be influenced, the most frequently mentioned behaviors are that the leader "supported me," "challenged me," "listened to me," "celebrated good work," "trusted me," "empowered others," "shared the project vision," "admitted mistakes," "advised others," "taught well," and "was patient." These are desired universal traits that cross all borders.

All these comments are about serving others and making others feel important, not about making the project manager look important. They are about empowering others, not about grabbing power. Project managers must be consistent and work hard—that is the preferred way to overcome project obstacles. Maintaining credibility requires passion, persistence, and patience, especially in the face of adversity. Often the lessons are learned the hard way, and admired leaders are ones who admit mistakes and learn from their experiences. Experts James Kouzes and Barry Posner (1993) identify six practices that they call the six "disciplines of credibility." Here is how to adapt them for use by project sponsors:

1. *Explore yourself.* Explore your inner territory. Look into the mirror and ask yourself questions like "Who am I?" "What do I believe in?" "What do I stand for?" To be credible as an executive, clarify your own values and beliefs. Once you are clear on your own values, translate them into a set of guiding principles that you communicate to the team you want to lead.

2. *Be sensitive with team members.* Understand that your own leadership philosophy is only the beginning. Being a leader also requires developing a deep understanding of the values and desires of team members. Listen to them. Leadership is a relationship, and you will only be able to build that relationship on mutual understanding and respect. Team members come to believe in their leaders—to see them as worthy of their trust—when they believe that the leaders have the team's best interests at heart.

3. *Confirm shared values.* Credible leaders honor the diversity of team members. They also find a common ground for agreement on which everyone can stand. They bring people together and join them in a cause. Project sponsors show others how everyone's individual values and interests can be served by coming to consensus on

a set of common values. Confirm a core of shared values passionately, and speak enthusiastically on behalf of the project.

4. *Develop capacity*. It is essential for project sponsors to develop
continuously the capacity of their members to keep their commitments. Ensure that educational opportunities exist for individuals
to build their knowledge and skill.

5. *Serve a purpose*. Leadership is a service. Project sponsors
serve a purpose for their people who have made it possible for them
to lead—their teams.

6. *Sustain hope*. Credible leaders keep hope alive. Teams need
a positive attitude from their leaders in troubling times of transition.
Optimists are proactive and behave in ways that promote health
and combat illness. People with high hope are also high achievers.

Project team members expect their leaders to have the courage
of their convictions. They expect them to stand up for their beliefs.
If leaders are not clear about what they believe in, they are much
more likely to change positions with every fad or opinion poll.
Without core beliefs and with only shifting positions, would-be
leaders will be judged as inconsistent and be derided for being "political" in their behavior.

Managers expect project managers to lead successful projects
and achieve good results. Credibility is a condition for project success that must be earned day by day during the project.

## Insights from Clifford Cohen, IT Manager

Few people really know why the sponsor is considered the sponsor
and why it is important to understand exactly why the person's
role—and the reason for that role—need to be clear. Whenever I
found myself talking to a "user champion" who thought he was a
sponsor, I quickly corrected the situation by identifying a sponsor
and clarifying the extent of the user champion's responsibilities. If
I was in a meeting and someone referred to anyone as a sponsor
who was not one by definition, I reminded everyone why this was

inappropriate and ultimately deleterious to the success of the project. If one person was assuming both roles, I would deal with him as if he were two different people. I never mixed discussion appropriate for one role with that for another role. I would meet with the individual and discuss project status, strategic direction, personnel issues, risks, and other sponsorship matters in one meeting and raise system requirement and functionality issues in another one.

This constant and strict adherence to role clarity was perhaps the single most effective thing I brought to troubled projects. My sponsors welcomed this clarity and moderated their input and influence accordingly, based on the situation once they saw the wisdom of it. The bottom line with me was that only through such diligence was it possible to ensure that all key roles were being played and being played right. In every case, my first action on taking over a troubled project was to clarify roles. My doing so never failed to impress both the business side and the technical side and made my job much easier from the outset.

## Summary

This chapter addresses the sponsorship role in the very specific form of a project-based organization in which providers conduct projects on behalf of clients. Extra effort is required to build and maintain successful relationships. That includes gathering information about each other, talking frequently, and following through on commitments.

Expectations are high in these business transactions. Know that clients want active and sustaining participation from the provider sponsor throughout the project life cycle. Find out specifically how clients want their needs met. Focus on ensuring that excellence in project sponsorship is a competitive advantage that keeps customers wanting to do business with you. Commit to exploring your values and behaviors that gain the credibility required for successful relationships.

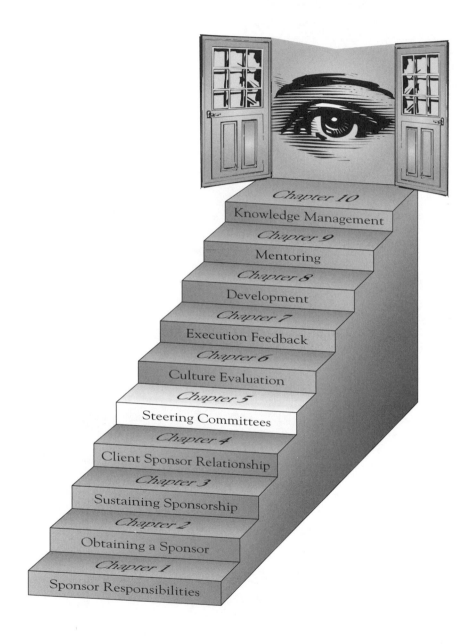

Chapter 10
Knowledge Management

Chapter 9
Mentoring

Chapter 8
Development

Chapter 7
Execution Feedback

Chapter 6
Culture Evaluation

Chapter 5
Steering Committees

Chapter 4
Client Sponsor Relationship

Chapter 3
Sustaining Sponsorship

Chapter 2
Obtaining a Sponsor

Chapter 1
Sponsor Responsibilities

# 5

# PLANNING AND EXECUTING STEERING COMMITTEES

> Our ultimate freedom is the right and power to
> decide how anybody or anything outside us will
> affect us.
>
> —*Stephen Covey*

A project is unlikely to succeed without an effective steering committee. The steering committee (sometimes called a project board or business team) is an organism whose mission is to help complete each project successfully. The relationship between a project and a steering committee is similar to the relationship between the board of directors and a company. There may even be a hierarchy of committees from project up to program and system. The purpose of the steering committee is to direct the project, not to manage it. As a former CEO at Hewlett-Packard replied in response to how a project management council could be more effective, "Make decisions!" Steering committees as a group need to agree on the problem and work together in deciding on the best solution. All participants need to be clear about their roles and responsibilities as well as the time frame under the new action, work plan, or strategy. It is also important to check outcomes regularly against measurable objectives or indicators to see if the solution has worked and whether the strategy needs to be revised or restarted.

Projects continue from one stage to the next because sponsors choose to continue or not continue spending resources. Instead of sponsors making these decisions unilaterally or on a whim, it is better to work with a steering committee whose goal is to ensure that each project continues to meet the needs of the organization.

This chapter covers the process of staffing, organizing, and conducting a steering committee as an extension of project sponsorship.

## Staffing

All executives in a company who represent business areas that are directly or indirectly involved in the project should belong to the project steering committee. For example, an organizational change project will have input from sales, marketing, human resources, operations, technology, and other project stakeholders. Therefore, senior management people from each of these areas need to be represented on the project steering committee.

What would be the ideal membership of a steering committee? Our recommendation is to establish representation from all main project stakeholders. In that way, all opinions, inputs, and feedback are taken into account in making decisions. A C-level manager (CEO, COO, CIO, CPO) may be involved to support the concept and staff these teams. The steering committee also works extremely closely with the project office, especially with regard to decisions involving project prioritization and resource allocation.

Individual steering committee members are not directly responsible for managing project activities but are responsible for providing support and guidance for those who do. Here's what steering committee members need to do:

- Understand the strategic implications and outcomes of initiatives being pursued through project outputs
- Appreciate the significance of the project for some or all major stakeholders and perhaps represent their interests
- Be genuinely interested in the initiative and the outcomes being pursued

- Advocate for the project's outcomes by being committed to and actively involved in pursuing the project's outcomes
- Have a broad understanding of project management issues and the approach being adopted

In practice, this means they need to do all the following things:

- Ensure that the project's outputs meet the requirements of the business owners and key stakeholders
- Help balance conflicting priorities and resources
- Provide guidance to the project team and users of the project's outputs
- Consider ideas and issues raised
- Foster positive communication outside of the committee regarding the project's progress and outcomes
- Review the progress of the project
- Check adherence of project activities against standards of best practices both within the organization and in a wider context
- Make decisions and enforce them

An IT project may be tempted to limit membership to its own function. However, most IT projects support business areas, and those business areas therefore need to have staffing involvement on steering committees to guide and validate project efficacy.

## Organizing

Organizing a project steering committee is essential for project success. Figure 5.1 represents an overall view of strategic project management. Steering committees play a key role linking projects to the rest of the pyramid through their function as a portfolio planning team.

## Figure 5.1  Strategic Project Management

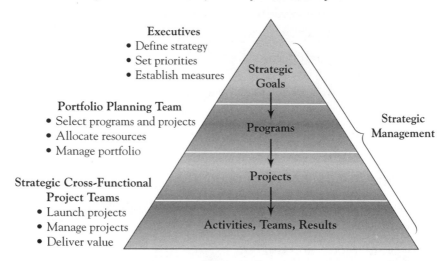

Here are a few rules to consider:

*Direction.* A project steering committee mandates and provides ongoing direction to the project manager. The steering committee takes responsibility for the project's feasibility, business plan, and achievement of outcomes.

*Empowerment.* The project steering committee empowers the project manager to undertake the project. It is also the committee's responsibility to ensure that the project manager receives all the assistance and resources required from various business units in order to deliver the project successfully as mandated. The project steering committee provides those directly involved in the project with guidance on project business issues.

*Control.* Every project needs to be under control. Consider operating within "bounded instability" wherein project teams operate on their own most of the time in what appears chaotic but is actually an effective creative process. Establish measures that set boundaries or early warning of problems, such as number of deliverables not met. The project manager is responsible for project success, but it is the responsibility of the steering committee to decide on and implement control mechanisms that monitor ongoing project status. Project overrun is not necessarily failure, but overrun without the knowledge of the steering committee is. The project steering committee ensures that efforts and expenditures are appropriate to stakeholder expectations.

*Decision making.* Certain decisions during the project life cycle cannot be made within the project team; they need to be escalated to the steering committee and possibly from there to the board of directors. The steering committee addresses any issue that has major implications for the project. For example, I (Bucero) managed a project in a savings bank where we engaged a third party to deliver services such as new processes, new organizational behavior models, and communication tools. That outside provider did not perform well, but I could not make the decision to fire it. I escalated that problem to the project steering committee, asking that the committee make a decision. The outside provider had been working for the savings bank for a long time, and firing the company risked affecting other customer areas. That privileged information was known only by some executives belonging to the steering committee, which ultimately decided to retain the outside provider. The steering committee resolved that the larger organizational relationship has higher priority than performance on a specific project.

## Acting as a Team

The project steering committee includes representatives of corporate clients, the project sponsor or sponsors, the business owner or owners, and sometimes the project manager. Usually, the members of the steering committee are not directly responsible for managing project activities but provide support and guidance for those who do. Upper managers through their roles on a steering committee can model desired organizational behaviors with regard to teamwork by demonstrating how teams collaborate to set strategy, prioritize, and decide issues. Members need to understand the strategic implications and outcomes of initiatives being pursued through projects; they need to appreciate the significance of each project for some or all major stakeholders. Membership also allows individuals or organizations to ensure representation of their interests.

The individuals belonging to the project steering committee must care about the initiative and the outcomes the project will produce. They are advocates for the project's outcomes. Steering committee members need to have a broad understanding of project management issues and the approach being adopted. Working as a team on the project steering committee is the basis for steering committee success and ultimately for project success.

For example, in a project I (Bucero) managed in a banking organization, I demonstrated to steering committee members that they could help me communicate and sell the project to various stakeholders. This worked well because they felt more involved in the project implementation.

In practice, this means that steering committee members perform the following tasks:

- Ensure that the requirements of project stakeholders are met by the project's outputs
- Help balance conflicting priorities and resources
- Provide guidance to the project team and users of the project's outputs
- Consider ideas and issues raised
- Review the progress of the project and see if some past good practices can be applied in the project

## Acting on Findings

By attending steering committees meetings, the project manager learns a lot from the attendees, their reactions, and their behaviors. At the beginning of one project I (Bucero) handled, steering committee members were very quiet, listening to me and appearing supportive. As the project progressed, however, I observed that they had a difficult time coming to decisions. I wrote meeting minutes with action plans after each meeting, yet at the next meeting, the same actions were still pending. Much discussion occurred during those meetings. Every attendee defended his or her particular interests, leading to even more discussion. Most meetings lasted around four hours because attendees did not respect the agenda and discussed too many things not focused on interests relevant to the project.

I first prepared a report that I distributed at the beginning of each meeting. I soon discovered that my report was too long and detailed. As the purpose of the steering committee was to make right decisions as soon as possible, I condensed the project status report to three slides only:

- Slide 1: Successes of This Period
    Deliverables finished
    Documentation finished
- Slide 2: Problems and Issues
    Important issues and problems
    Escalation
- Slide 3: Action Plan
    Action 1. Owner: AB. Date: dd/mm/yy
    Action 2. Owner: RE. Date: dd/mm/yy
    Action 3. Owner: . . .

Meeting times fell dramatically. The meetings were much more effective, and people felt more comfortable. Action taking improved. Gradually, I received a much higher level of commitment from each steering committee member.

This process took months, but it was worth it. Fewer discussions were required, and we focused on solving and taking actions that were relevant for the project.

Another way to take action on findings is to address the lessons learned from project reviews and retrospectives. A best practice recommendation is for the steering committee to require each project manager at the beginning of the project to review prior work and then make a presentation to the committee. Areas to cover include what was learned, what applies to this project, what can be adapted for this project, and what practices or risks should be avoided. This action by a steering committee is perhaps a far better knowledge management system than any other more extensive effort could be. Steering committees are in an ideal position to effect the principles of a learning organization (see Senge and others, 1994).

## Demonstrating Desired Behaviors

Members' behavior on steering committees depends on the type of project and organization. Different cultures imply different behaviors. The objective for steering committee members is to work together on a team for project success, but sometimes, especially at the beginning of a project, conflicting interests come up and generate problems among participants.

What do you look for? Every steering committee member needs to think and act in accordance with what would be best for project and organizational success, regardless of personal and professional interests. That is easy to say but difficult to implement.

Collaborative behaviors make for a productive and effective steering committee. The project manager needs support from the steering committee. This requires that the project manager keep the steering committee updated and informed periodically about progress, status, problems, and issues. The project sponsor—who adds perspective about the project, business, and environment—can support the project manager by extending and validating the communications. If committee members do not work well together, that sets the tone for the entire project, as well as for the organization in general. If teamwork is a desired practice for the organization, the starting point is steering committee members acting together as a team. That means they meet regularly, make decisions, and convey a consistent message. They are the drivers for implementing strategy. To do so requires understanding, and taking action in ways that all involved agree fulfill strategic goals.

Getting project steering committee members to behave in the desired ways is not easy. Members are drawn from different organizational areas and need to spend time together to bring their mission and objectives into alignment.

## Executive Testimonials

Rick Belluzzo (2003) is chairman of the board and chief executive officer of Quantum Corporation in San Jose, California, a global leader in high-tech storage products that meet demanding requirements for data integrity and availability. His experiences make him an expert on how to manage, lead, and succeed in a challenging and fast-moving industry and are especially appropriate for steering committees.

> I have been able to work for a number of companies, developing products and markets for exciting new technology. These technological developments and new products often failed their original intentions, but in almost every case, these efforts led to new insights and innovations that in some ways changed the world we live in. In other cases, they created the opportunity for growth and economic development. . . .
>
> These are very difficult times for many companies and their employees. But I am incredibly optimistic about the future and believe that most of the elements for success are not dramatic new strategies or complex, big mergers. Instead, we can only make our businesses successful if we prioritize the critical essentials that made our companies great in the first place. We must always strive to innovate and make a contribution better than any of the competitors. So take a risk on innovation. Next, whatever innovation you have depends on great people doing their best work. Don't try to motivate or micromanage your team. Hire great people, give them clear direction, and then work to eliminate the barriers to success. Work together at all levels of management to implement these practices. Finally, remember that customers are the only reason we build businesses. Once you get them, do everything possible to keep them satisfied. In fact, try to shift more investment into supporting your customers. It will have an impact.
>
> These are principles I follow in order to allow my company to be a vital element of an exciting and growing industry. Getting back

to these fundamentals is the only way to once again have a thriving and growing economy.

Joe Eng is CIO of the Society for Worldwide Interbank Financial Telecommunication (Swift), an industry-owned cooperative that supplies messaging services and software used by most of the world's banks to send daily financial transactions. He "set new performance standards for his IT department, negotiated technical requirements with demanding business partners, calmed nervous end users, and built a $500 million global network by following four simple principles" (Holmes, 2005).

*Principle 1: Define Expectations Internally.* Eng set as his first task making sure his staff understood why new messaging technology was needed and how they would approach designing, building and deploying it. . . . Eng assembled a cadre of senior and middle managers from throughout the company whom he thought employees admired and trusted. If these managers bought into a common approach to the project, the staff would take their cues from them. The debates about technology and deployment strategies would be minimized.

"I needed these vanguards out there in the company selling the idea of change because I spent a lot of my time working with executive management, the board and customers," Eng says. . . . The expectation was set: When problems cropped up, the IT team would manage them and learn from them without letting the project get derailed. . . . Rather than measuring the amount of time spent on specific tasks, managers would measure the results of the work.

*Principle 2: Establish Rules of Engagement.* Most customers felt strongly that they needed everything they wanted. . . . Rather than debating every idea with every customer, Eng decided to develop SwiftNet through pilots with a subset of representative customers. Whatever functionality was built into the pilots became the basis for SwiftNet's requirements. The pilot customers understood what to expect from the system because they had been involved in deciding what they would get. They could then effectively manage the expectations of other customers by becoming public supporters of the system they helped build.

*Principle 3: Deal with Doubters.* As the day approached to launch the pilot, executives were getting nervous and began to second-guess whether the network would be as reliable as promised. One of the bigger customer groups wanted to clarify responsibilities for the project and asked Eng to meet with them. "There would have been no second chance if it could not be shown that the end-to-end system worked effectively," said the chief operating officer. . . . Eng made himself aware of the source of confusion, saying, "I didn't want to be surprised, and I wanted to be honest and stick to the facts." The executives were satisfied, saying, "Joe showed a sense of pragmatism and goodwill to find the way forward in what otherwise could have been a difficult circumstance."

*Principle 4: Not Everything Is Negotiable.* Banks had to follow a complicated process to migrate to SwiftNet that included deploying a pilot before they would be ready for full operation. Slowing down the rollout was not an option. . . . Eng's original plan was to assign countries to "windows," in which smaller customers in each country or region had a set time to migrate to SwiftNet. Large customers had their own migration schedules. To make up for lost time, Eng devoted additional resources to quality assurance before the migration began. In addition, his staff found ways to add the large customers to each country window or overlap the beginning and end of each window so that more banks were migrating at a time. . . . Eng was innovative in identifying solutions. Eng and the IT department succeeded and earned credibility by effectively managing stakeholder expectations.

Mark Tonnesen is vice president of sales operations for customer advocacy at Cisco Systems, Inc., in San Jose, California. Here are his key thoughts about steering committees.

An organization never has enough resources to accomplish their desired road map. So you need to make decisions. Some key questions:

Where do we make the big bets?

Where do we place our resources?

How do we determine the priorities?

Road map planning sessions with business stakeholders are required to make rational decisions around these questions.

Rosemary Hossenlopp, principal consultant for Project Management Perspectives LLC in San Jose, California, who has worked with VP Tonnesen at Cisco, shared her thoughts on an issue about communicating with upper management teams that she feels strongly about.

> Become a recognized expert on your team. There is a fundamental problem that affects almost every technical project team member: you have limited access to senior management. If your role is positioned only as a team member, you may be perceived as a commodity.
>
> There is a way that you can get noticed by sponsors. There is a way to win customer confidence when you speak. It requires that you have a clear idea of the value case that the business wants to achieve. Everything you say must help the business understand how you and the technology team can help the organization perform against those objectives. If customers and sponsors know you as a person who speaks their business language, you can then move from team member to a position of team leadership.

## Tools with Examples

Use time at steering committee sessions to discuss issues that face the attendees:

- Tensions and cooperation
- Projects as illustrations of larger issues
- Effective use of time
- Outside issues that affect the project
- Resolve cross-organizational disputes or behaviors

Exhibit 5.1 provides a form that can be used to document activity and highlight issues that need to come to the attention of the steering committee. It serves as a real-time dashboard. It also functions over time to distill lengthy meeting minutes down to essential issues addressed by the group.

## Exhibit 5.1  Project Status Report

**Project Status Report for Executive Committee and Project Sponsor**

Project Name: _____

Project Sponsor: _____

Project Manager: _____

| Reporting Period: | Monthly/Quarterly/Weekly | Date: | |
|---|---|---|---|

Risk Status Alert Indicator

| | Low | Medium | High | Change |
|---|---|---|---|---|
| Scope | | | | |
| Schedule | | | | |
| Budget | | | | |

Changes to Project Plan

| Describe Change | Approved | Date |
|---|---|---|
| | | |
| | | |

Political Issues

| Describe Issue | Importance | Recommendations |
|---|---|---|
| | | |
| | | |

Schedule Status (Milestones and Deliverables to Be Met in Next Reporting Period)

| |
|---|
| |
| |
| |

Budget Status                                        Above or Below Budget (%)

| Project Budget | $ | |
|---|---|---|
| Actual Spending to Date | $ | |
| Est. to Complete | $ | |

---

**Exhibit 5.1  Project Status Report, Cont'd**

---

Comments:

```
┌─────────────────────────────────────────────────────┐
│                                                     │
│                                                     │
│                                                     │
│                                                     │
│                                                     │
│                                                     │
│                                                     │
└─────────────────────────────────────────────────────┘
```

Signed _____   Date _____

---

# Steering Committee Checklist

Answering the following questions can be very useful to the company's sponsor and project manager in planning and executing regular project steering committee meetings:

1. Are the steering committee's objectives clear?

2. Do we have a clear and time-scheduled meeting agenda?

3. Have all participants been informed of the meeting and given the proposed agenda with required preparatory material indicated?

4. Has the client sponsor been briefed and invited?

5. Were briefings with key decision makers scheduled and conducted before the steering committee meeting?

6. Are plans, including those for resources and financials, up to date and presentable?

7. Have decisions required of the steering committee been properly documented and communicated?

8. Have the next steering committee meetings been scheduled?

## Summary

Excellence in project sponsorship extends beyond an individual's responsibility. It involves a broad base of support of representatives across the organization that has a stake in the outcome, brought together in the steering committee. They commit to work together. Their work consists of reviewing progress, making decisions, and taking action. An effective steering committee ensures that the project links to and meets strategic goals. The committee is also an effective means, through its actions, to demonstrate desired behaviors and guide a learning organization.

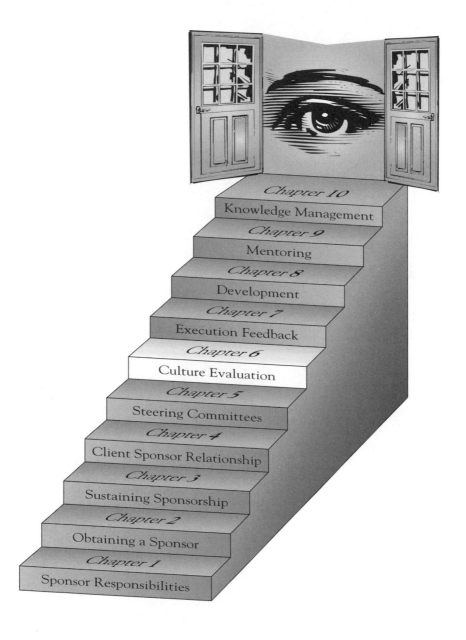

Chapter 10
Knowledge Management

Chapter 9
Mentoring

Chapter 8
Development

Chapter 7
Execution Feedback

Chapter 6
Culture Evaluation

Chapter 5
Steering Committees

Chapter 4
Client Sponsor Relationship

Chapter 3
Sustaining Sponsorship

Chapter 2
Obtaining a Sponsor

Chapter 1
Sponsor Responsibilities

# 6

# SPONSORSHIP AND CULTURE EVALUATION

> Human beings, by changing the inner attitudes of their
> minds, can change the outer aspects of their lives.
> —*William James*

Every project can be considered as creating a change. What happens during that change process? Usually, we find conflicts and resistance. It is natural that as human beings working in organizations, we find positive forces like motivating challenges, strong sponsors, and driving groups. We also find negative forces like organizational resistance, management layers, and individual resistance. Some potential sources of resistance in projects managed in organizations are the following:

- Lack of knowledge and motivation
- Low will or desire
- Nonalignment of goals
- Different values and beliefs
- Lack of upper management direction

Culture may be described as the way we do things in organizations, including "war stories," symbols, rituals, shared values, power structures, traditions and norms, and styles. Being conscious of the culture in an organization is a step toward making necessary changes.

The chapter reviews the types of culture often experienced in project-based organizations and the roles required to manage change, especially when sponsorship practices need to improve. We discuss the sponsor's financial responsibility role, which is not only a major area of contribution but also a sticky area when differing values cause problems. We offer survey and assessment forms that help evaluate the current reality. These set the stage for putting risk mitigation plans into place that foster a culture of excellence in sponsorship.

## Corporate Cultures

A first step is to understand the cultural environment. Corporate culture may be classified by type: an organization can have a power, bureaucratic, task-oriented, or person-oriented culture.

*Power culture:* A single person or small group leads the organization. There is little or no respect for formal structures and procedures. Often these organizations are entrepreneurial. When these organizations grow, they have adaptation problems. This culture is very often difficult to change.

*Bureaucratic culture:* All things are done following the rules. People place high value on loyalty. Political success comes from knowing how to play the system.

*Task-oriented culture:* The organization is built around temporary project teams. It relies on people playing fairly. The problem is that situations can easily break down into vicious political infighting.

*Person-oriented culture:* Each individual follows his or her own interests. Members have mutually beneficial links to other members.

Sponsorship roles may be quite clear in power and bureaucratic cultures when power and rules are vested in sponsors as a matter of course. A project-based organization prospers in a task-oriented culture; here the sponsor role needs careful delineation and implementation—the task being set out in this book. Sponsorship probably encounters its greatest challenge in a person-oriented culture because of the difficulties in getting people to support organizational goals. Assess and use your organization's culture orientation as a guide for subsequent actions.

## Critical Roles

Everyone has roles to perform in a change management process. Clients request projects, and projects generate changes in organizations. Those changes usually affect people, methods, processes, and products. There are four critical roles in organizations that run projects (see Figure 6.1): *advocates* want change but do not have the organizational power to sponsor it themselves, *sponsors* have the authority to commit resources, *agents* carry out the change, and *targets* receive or adjust to the change. Change agents need to plan, understand the culture, and proactively create synergy; identify who will be affected by the change; and passionately build a vision that people will adopt because they believe in it.

The project sponsor needs to demonstrate strong commitment to the project. If the sponsor commitment is low, the risk of implementation failure increases.

### Figure 6.1  Roles in Change Management

Sponsorship is critical to successful change and cannot be delegated to agents. "Initiating" and "sustaining" sponsors are advised not to fulfill each other's functions. Educate or replace weak sponsors, or failure is inevitable.

Famous words from the sixteenth century still ring true today:

> There is nothing more difficult to take in hand, more perilous to conduct, or more uncertain in this success than to take the lead in the new order of things. For he who innovates will have for his enemies all those who have prospered under the old order, and only lukewarm supporters in those who might be better off under the new. This lukewarmness arises partly from fear of their adversaries who have the laws in their favor, and partly from the incredulity of [humans], who do not truly believe in anything new until they have had actual experience of it [Machiavelli, *The Prince*, 1537].

The best chance for achieving management commitment to project success occurs when people clearly understand and embrace what success is and see the cause-and-effect contribution of excellence in project sponsorship. Success breeds success. But until sponsorship is recognized as a core competence, making changes follows a difficult path. People advance on this path when all players accept their interdependent roles and make the commitment to accountability.

## Financial Responsibilities

More than any other player, the sponsor, depending on the organization, has specific responsibilities for project funding. Strengths and weaknesses here correlate directly with project success and failure.

Clifford Cohen, former IT manager and now project management consultant, says:

> The sponsor is the person who controls the money that is paying for a project. He or she is not the user champion (the system expert and

key source of system requirements), the performing organization, miscellaneous stakeholders, or any other persons/roles related to project execution. The sponsor controls the purse strings. End of story. This is the key to the sponsor's power and influence in the project equation. . . . In short, the only person on a project who I feel has the right to provide guidance of the type typically reserved for sponsors is the person who controls the purse strings. If they don't know how to provide the guidance, they shouldn't be controlling the money. People who don't control the money shouldn't be trusted to correctly perform the sponsorship role. No matter how responsible and savvy they may be, it isn't their money; and therefore they will invariably make at least one or two wrong decisions because of this.

Financial responsibilities characterize client sponsors. The financial reasons for the project and the return on investment that the customer organization expects to achieve are perspectives that receive much attention. Sometimes the customer is only the owner of the project. This may hold true for contracted work but may not hold true for projects geared toward serving internal needs such as network upgrades and database development.

Our experience in new product development in the high tech industry reveals that sponsors focus less on cost tracking and more on head count. It is a given that products need to be developed and money will be spent on those activities. Budgets are based on how many people are assigned to each project.

Similarly, in financial institutions that he has worked with, J. Davidson Frame, noted author and Fellow of the Project Management Institute, notes that project budgets are defined not in monetary terms but in level of effort terms—body counts over time. As each project is reviewed by a project selection panel during the business case and project selection phase, the project champion may ask for one tester to serve two weeks on the project, two Java programmers to serve three weeks each, and so forth. These are IT projects carried out within the organization, especially since the majority of IT projects implemented by financial services companies address internal IT needs. Since 95 percent of project budgets are tied up in human resources, it is not necessary to monitor dollar budgets closely.

Frame further notes that when work is contracted out, the sponsor role needs to reflect the realities of contracting. This case likely focuses heavily on budgets. On cost-plus contracts, the contractor will be held accountable for what it bills the client, so the sponsor needs to be able to justify expenses and make sure costs do not get out of hand. On fixed-price contracts, every dollar wasted is a dollar deducted from profit.

## Owner Versus Sponsor Roles

Frame also expresses strong beliefs about roles, albeit from a slightly different perspective. He says:

> A few years ago when I was actively working with [a number of] financial companies (most IT groups, but not always), each of these organizations straightened me out about the difference between project sponsors and owners.
>
> Owners are the folks who own the results and who usually pay the bills. You don't want them guiding the project team, because they have an inherent conflict of interest—their primary concern is to get the results they need (as owners). Their bonuses may be tied to the results. So they will pressure the team to do whatever is necessary so that their personal goals are achieved—even when this may run against the interest of the organization (for example, they may encourage corner cutting).
>
> Sponsors, in contrast, are senior managers who simultaneously serve the Executive Committee (that is, the governing committee of the company who—theoretically—are guardians of the organization's interests) and the needs of the team. Because they are powerful, they do everything they can to make sure that the project achieves

visibility among senior managers and that it gets the resources it needs. At the same time, they make sure the team is behaving competently and serving the organization's needs. If the team is drifting away from the targets established by senior management, or if they feel team members are sloppy, etc., they pull out their clubs and smack a couple of heads. Unlike project owners, they don't have a personal stake in the results—their bonuses and job security are not tied to project performance. This means they can maintain a degree of objectivity lacking in owners.

Cohen responds:

I understand the distinction that David is making—absolutely valid. My view of sponsorship is very simple in a way, but it has served me well: if people are paying for something, they get what they want—period (subject to typical project constraints). Their control of the money means that they are the ultimate authorities as to what happens on the project. The users are relied on to define what is desired, and the sponsor ignores their input at great risk to the organization, but issues surrounding strategic justification for the project, prioritization, issue resolution, high-level advocacy, and so on are within the province of the sponsor. I believe it is at least partly the responsibility of the PM to ensure that sponsors, who are also owners, behave as sponsors while acting in that role. I go back to the fact that if they have been given control of the money, they have been entrusted to perform in the best interests of the organization and should be relied on to lead the project. If this does not occur, they should not be the sponsors. But if the wrong person is chosen as a sponsor, his or her failure and that of the project ultimately rests with those who assigned the role. At the end of the day, the success of an organization depends on the ability of more senior management to understand the criticality of such decisions.

Cohen and Frame appear to offer conflicting approaches. However, each has validity, depending on the situation. Within product development organizations, for example, the sponsor needs to drive the funding situation. As organizations and projects get larger, financial limits may be set, such as funding approval up to $1 million projects. This sponsor must go higher to get approval for a $1.4 million project. Accountability and authority may not match, but that should not be an excuse for not actively managing the role.

## Sponsor Risk Assessment

Before implementing a project, it is crucial to measure the readiness for project implementation. An overall environmental assessment survey instrument (EASI) is available on the Web in the "Offerings" section of http://www.englundpmc.com. EASI relates specifically to each component of *Creating an Environment for Successful Projects* (Graham and Englund, 2004). The environmental assessment may point to specific areas of strengths and development opportunities.

In Exhibit 6.1, we introduce a risk assessment survey to raise the awareness of the organization's current positioning for the change caused by the project. This tool provides a high-level analysis of possible risk areas for the planned project. It thus allows you to know more about the situation and the attitudes of the people involved. Risk is assessed on the basis of eight critical factors for any change: motivation, commitment, shared vision, culture, alignment, communication, planning, and skills.

Use this tool with all project stakeholders, possibly with different layers in the organization and with various groups. In that way, you collect contrasted opinions to check the issues found. Report survey results back to all participants in a sensitive way. Figure 6.2 provides a graphical means to summarize risk assessment scores. A tight grouping around low scores indicates low maturity and high risk. Jagged scores—some high and some low—helps pinpoint areas of strengths and development needs.

## Exhibit 6.1  Risk Assessment Survey

**Instructions**

The following items reflect the key elements of risk assessment. Rate each element on a scale from 1 to 5, with 1 = "disagree strongly," 2 = "disagree somewhat," 3 = "neither agree nor disagree," 4 = "agree somewhat," and 5 = "agree strongly."

1.  Motivation for the Project                                          Score

1.1  There is a convincing business need for the project.              _____

1.2  There are significant risks to the business if the project       _____
     is unsuccessful.

1.3  The level of dissatisfaction with the current situation is       _____
     mutually shared by employees and management.

1.4  There is a sense of urgency to change felt by everyone.          _____

1.5  The extent of the impact on those affected by the               _____
     project (in terms of work habits, power, and security) is
     minimal.

TOTAL                                                                 _____

2.  Commitment to the Project

2.1  There is publicly committed sponsorship for the change.          _____

2.2  Resources, time, and money are committed to sustain the         _____
     change.

2.3  The sponsor is at a high enough level in the organization to     _____
     have decision-making authority.

2.4  The parties implementing the change are considered credible      _____
     by the parties affected by the change.

2.5  The sponsor clearly understands his or her responsibility,       _____
     especially when conflict arises.

2.6  There is a guiding coalition (other leaders supporting the       _____
     sponsor) to drive the project.

2.7  First-line managers actively support the change.                 _____

TOTAL                                                                 _____

## Exhibit 6.1  Risk Assessment Survey, Cont'd

3.  Shared Vision of the Project

3.1  There is a tight link between the vision for the project and        _____
the organization's overall vision.

3.2  People can relate the vision for the change to themselves        _____
personally in a positive way.

3.3  There is a well-articulated vision of the change that is        _____
commonly understood and shared by all stakeholders.

3.4  There is a strong leadership to sustain the vision for the change.    _____

3.5  The vision statement is clear, convincing, and compelling.        _____

TOTAL        _____


4.  Cultural Match with the Project

4.1  The project aligns with the culture of the organization.        _____

4.2  The implementation approach is appropriate to the        _____
organizational culture.

4.3  The strength of the culture is likely to reinforce the change        _____
direction.

4.4  Previous changes have been handled well in this organization.    _____

4.5  Decision making is timely and implemented.        _____

4.6  There is a high degree of trust between managers and        _____
employees in the areas affected by the change.

TOTAL        _____


5.  Organizational Alignment

5.1  Planning cycles support project resource requirements.        _____

5.2  Reward structures encourage adoption of the change by all        _____
affected parties.

5.3  Processes support the sustainability of the change.        _____

5.4  Consequences are articulated and followed through on.        _____

5.5  Management practices and behavior support the change.        _____

5.6  There is a manageable level of stress in the organization.        _____

TOTAL        _____

## Exhibit 6.1  Risk Assessment Survey, Cont'd

6. Communication

6.1  The organization uses three-way communication.      _____

6.2  Communication generally reaches and is understood at all levels.      _____

6.3  The communication plan is comprehensive and timely.      _____

6.4  Multiple media are available for communicating in this organization.      _____

6.5  The magnitude of the change is small both vertical and horizontally.      _____

TOTAL      _____

7. Transition Planning

7.1  There is a transition plan in place that allows adequate time for the change.      _____

7.2  The transition plan is comprehensive, covering human, process, and technical dimensions.      _____

7.3  Transition measures are incorporated into the plan.      _____

7.4  Potential problems and risks have been identified, and plans are in place for resolving them quickly.      _____

7.5  The implementation approach is aligned with the scope of the change (time frames, methods, degree of involvement).      _____

TOTAL      _____

8. Skills

8.1  The change agents have sound skills for implementing the change process.      _____

8.2  Those affected by the change have the technical and job skills necessary to perform the new activities.      _____

8.3  People understand their personal transitioning process.      _____

8.4  There are suitable mentors available to help people through the change.      _____

8.5  Employees have a sense of empowerment that is appropriate to the nature of the change.      _____

8.6  Teamwork is highly developed in this organization.      _____

TOTAL      _____

## Exhibit 6.1  Risk Assessment Survey, Cont'd

**Scoring Instructions**

1. Total the scores for each section (1 through 8).
2. Divide the section scores by the factor identified in the following table to obtain an adjusted score.

| Section | Score | Divisor | Adjusted Score |
|---|---|---|---|
| Motivation | | 5 | |
| Commitment | | 7 | |
| Shared vision | | 5 | |
| Culture | | 6 | |
| Alignment | | 6 | |
| Communication | | 5 | |
| Planning | | 5 | |
| Skills | | 6 | |

3. Total of adjusted scores _____
4. Multiply the total adjusted score by 2.5 to obtain an overall risk assessment score _____
5. Mark the range for your overall risk assessment:

   High/Danger (20–40) _____

   Moderate/Caution (41–70) _____

   Low/Opportunity (71–100) _____

6. Draw a spider diagram similar to the one shown in Figure 6.2 to show the main areas of risk. High scores indicate minimum risk, low scores require risk strategies.

## Figure 6.2  Radar Chart for Sponsor Risk Assessment Results

Sponsor Risk Assessment Chart

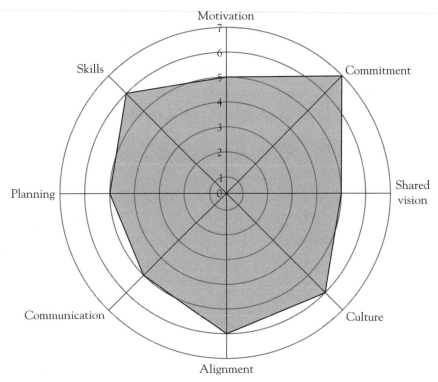

Nonsponsors can also complete the survey and use it to give structured feedback to the sponsor. Use these surveys as a data source for accelerating dialogue around project and sponsor processes as well as for providing feedback to the sponsor (feedback will be discussed at greater length in Chapter Seven).

## Sponsor Evaluation Tool

The sponsor evaluation tool in Exhibit 6.2 is designed to assess sponsor commitment for a specific project. Low levels of sponsor commitment increase the risk of implementation failure. Use this sponsor evaluation during initial project planning, before the project has been announced, anytime after the announcement has been made, and after project implementation is complete.

## Exhibit 6.2  Sponsor Evaluation Tool

**Instructions**

The following questions probe the key elements of sponsor commitment. Rate each question on a scale from 1 to 7, with 1 indicating a resounding no, 4 indicating indifference, and 7 indicating a resounding yes.

1. Is the sponsor dissatisfied with the way things are?  _____

2. Are the sponsor's goals for the project clear?  _____

3. Does the sponsor believe that there is a real need for the project?  _____

4. Does the sponsor understand the long-term impact the change will have on the organization?  _____

5. Does the sponsor understand what people are being asked to change about the way they operate?  _____

6. Does the sponsor understand how many people or groups will be affected by the project?  _____

7. Does the sponsor understand what resources are needed for the project to be successful?  _____

8. Is the sponsor willing to commit the resources needed for the project to succeed?  _____

9. Does the sponsor publicly convey the organization's strong commitment to change?  _____

10. Is the sponsor willing to meet privately with individuals or groups to convey strong personal support for the change?  _____

11. Will the sponsor use rewards and pressures to gain support for the project?  _____

12. Will the sponsor ensure that procedures to track progress and problems are established?  _____

13. Is the sponsor aware of the prices that must be paid for the project to succeed?  _____

14. Is the sponsor willing to make sacrifices to ensure the success of the project?  _____

15. Will the sponsor show consistent, sustained support for the project?  _____

## Exhibit 6.2  Sponsor Evaluation Tool, Cont'd

**Scoring**

The sponsor factor reflects the risk of implementation failure of a project. The lower the factor, the greater is the risk of implementation failure. To calculate your sponsor factor:

1. Total your responses for all items.

2. Divide the total by 15.

3. Divide by 7 and multiply the result by 100.

4. Check the range into which your sponsor factor falls:

   _____ High Risk/Danger (10–34)

   _____ Moderate/Caution (35–65)

   _____ Low Risk/Opportunity (66 and above)

See the text for a detailed analysis.

Why is it important to do this evaluation?

- To provide early warning for potential commitment problems and possible implementation failure
- To determine sponsor commitment toward the project
- To analyze possible differences in commitment during the implementation process
- To identify sponsor commitment that was generated after implementation

## Interpreting Sponsor Factor Scores

The sponsor factor reflects the risk of implementation failure of a project. The lower the factor, the greater the risk of implementation failure.

## High Risk/Danger (10-34)

Most projects with a score in this range fail to achieve full implementation. An exception may be when the sponsor does not consider the project to significantly alter the status quo. Nevertheless, a project that is significantly disruptive or potentially threatening needs to have a degree of sponsorship well above this score. Three options to consider when the sponsor factor scores in this range area:

*Strengthen sponsorship.* Use this instrument as an educational tool to help sponsors better understand and value the critical nature of their role.

*Identify alternative sponsorship.* If it is not possible to strengthen the existing sponsor support, identify some other person or group with the power to legitimize the project and secure that party's agreement to serve as the sponsor. David Frame points out that if the sponsor owns the project budget, it is not easy to do this readily. "It means, in effect, that you will be taking budget away from one person and transferring it to another. This may be perceived as a demotion of the original sponsor, which may have political repercussions if this individual is a senior VP." He goes on to ask, who will appoint the new sponsor? The project steering committee? The executive committee? The project manager? "I have encountered smaller IT projects where the PM is required to sweet-talk a senior manager into being the sponsor. If the sponsor does not participate in project activities—a common experience—then the PM needs to identify a new sponsor."

Companies like CEPSA (a Spanish petroleum company) specify in their PM methodology that if the sponsor assigned is not working properly, he or she must delegate all the power and authority to another manager. I (Bucero) have lived through such an experience in that organization, and it worked only when the initial sponsor asked for a meeting with all project steering committee members and formally delegated the sponsor's authority to a new manager.

*Prepare to fail.* Without strengthened sponsorship or new sponsorship, the probability of successful implementation is low. Facing these circumstances, the person in the change agent role (often a project or program manager) should consider aborting the change project or significantly altering the objectives so that new perspectives on the issues can develop. A PM with minimal influence or power may not be in a position to abort anything. If the project is chartered by senior management as part of a formal project launch process, the PM may not be able to abort the project or change the approved objectives. It is important for the change agent to be proactive. A PM needs to take action and at least propose something to the management team or steering committee. The PM can ask for a meeting. That way the management team cannot say that the project manager did not raise a red flag about the situation. If, for political reasons, there is pressure to continue the project without these alterations, make preparations to deal with the problems that will arise when the project fails to produce intended results.

## Moderate Risk/Caution (35-65)

Partial or tentative support from sponsors does not always result in implementation failure, but it does increase the chances of failure. It certainly means that implementation is more complicated. A sponsor factor in this range alerts you to the following possibilities:

- The sponsor may have an intellectual commitment to the change but fail to grasp the full meaning of what is necessary for successful implementation
- The sponsor support for the change could deteriorate rapidly and with little warning.
- A significant amount of time and effort will need to be invested in sponsor education and maintenance.

## Low Risk/Opportunity (66 and Above)

Sponsorship should never be taken for granted, but scores in this range generally indicate that the sponsor commitment is at a level necessary for successful change implementation.

Although the overall score is positive, any item with the score of 3 or less should not be ignored. Items scoring less than 3 are often problem areas requiring special attention. For scores in this range area, consider extending sponsorship opportunities.

Tap the sponsor abilities on new projects that come up. If the sponsor is already assigned the sponsorship role on new projects, the job is to reuse experiences and ensure that best practices are followed. If not officially assigned, the sponsor can provide guidance as an unofficial mentor. Even better for the organization and project success is to designate official mentors; use the expertise developed by persons who acted as sponsors to coach and influence others to adopt best practices.

## Interpreting the Results

Table 6.1 allows interpretation of the results for individual items. Any item in the low-risk range indicates a high level of sponsor commitment and a positive feeling for successful implementation. Any item in the moderate-risk range indicates a moderate level of sponsor commitment and a guarded feeling for successful implementation. Any item in the high-risk range indicates a low level of sponsor commitment and a negative feeling for successful implementation.

# Summary

People are still struggling in their attempts to define the role of sponsors and to reconcile their perceptions. Some people use the terms *sponsor* and *champion* interchangeably. Others use *sponsor* and *owner* interchangeably. David Frame notes that best practice enterprises are moving toward consensus along these lines:

> Sponsors are the bridge that connect the project work effort with the desires of senior managers. They concurrently serve two audiences. They serve the project team by doing what they can to make

**Table 6.1 Categorizing the Risk for Individual Items**

| Characteristics | Low Risk/ Opportunity (7, 6) | Moderate Risk/Caution (5, 4, 3) | High Risk/ Danger (2, 1) |
|---|---|---|---|
| Dissatisfaction | | | |
| Goals | | | |
| Need | | | |
| Organizational impact | | | |
| Human impact | | | |
| Scope | | | |
| Resources | | | |
| Resource commitment | | | |
| Public role | | | |
| Private role | | | |
| Consequence management | | | |
| Monitoring activities | | | |
| Awareness of sacrifice | | | |
| Commitment to sacrifice | | | |
| Sustained support | | | |

sure the team gets the support it needs to achieve project goals (including resources and visibility). And they serve senior managers by making sure that the team stays aligned with the goals established by senior managers and by reporting progress and concerns to senior managers.

However, when you look at the details of their activities and responsibilities, it is evident that they vary from enterprise to enterprise. In some enterprises, sponsors are super senior executives; in others, reasonably high level, experienced mentors (but not from the highest ranks of the organization). In some enterprises, they actively play a budget-monitoring role; in others, they do not. In some enterprises, they are appointed by senior managers; in others, by the project steering committee; in still others, they are recruited by the project manager. Beyond this, it is clear that the role of the sponsor will be different for projects that serve the internal needs of the organizations versus projects geared toward satisfying outside customers such as via contracts.

Colleague Tom Kendrick, writing about project risks (2003), identifies the crucial role of U.S. President Teddy Roosevelt in the completion of the Panama Canal. As a project sponsor who "dared mighty things," Roosevelt provided the most significant morale builder for the project. As the first president to leave the country, he sailed to Panama in 1906 and visited the project. On his return, so much was written about the magnitude and importance of the canal that interest and support spread quickly.

On the other hand, Kendrick says, "Politically, the most difficult situation on technical projects arises from the changes requested by sponsors and management. . . . The sponsor can lower risk for the project by aggressively removing organizational barriers and administrative overhead and by dealing with organizational and business factors that may inhibit fast execution of the project. Conversely, management can exacerbate risk by contributing to these factors and initiating new work that requires people currently asssigned to your project. Strong, continuing sponsorship is one of the key factors that separate risky projects that succeed from those that crash and burn."

This chapter defines roles for players in sponsoring projects in organizations. These people are managing change. Although a sponsor has a crucial role with regard to financial responsibility, the actual role and limits may vary, depending on the type of organization. We also highlight the role of corporate culture. The nature of the organization guides likelihood of success and how much work and time may be required to effect major change in how projects are

sponsored. Surveys and evaluation tools help clarify the current reality in the organization and assess the risks of proceeding with
project-based work. When risk is low, go full speed ahead, and use
the capacity generated by these practices to extend organizational
capabilities. Be cautious when risk is high. Find ways to educate
sponsors to address these topics or else scale back on project commitments to lessen the impact of failure.

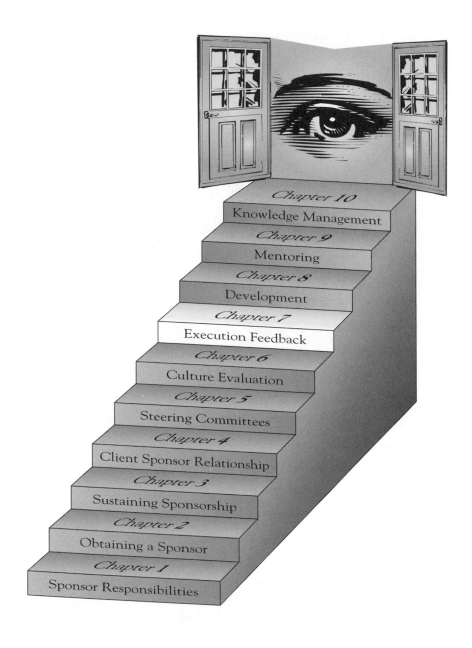

# 7

# SPONSORSHIP EXECUTION FEEDBACK

I hear and I forget. I see and I remember. I do and I understand.

*—Confucius*

To be assigned as project sponsor and execute that role during the project life cycle is not a one-shot deal. A key success factor in good sponsorship is communication. Feedback is part of the communication process. Communicating results is almost as important as achieving results.

By giving feedback to the project sponsor, stakeholders provide opportunities for the sponsor to change or improve actions, reactions, and behaviors. Sponsors are professionals who can benefit from listening to their teams and project stakeholders. Getting feedback as a sponsor may require active solicitation of others to share their experiences. It is important to receive the truths shared and make decisions based on inputs received. It is difficult to give feedback to power. Speaking the truth to power, especially bad news, is difficult most of the time but not impossible. Feedback is essential to ensure open and direct communication.

This chapter provides useful information for collecting feedback regarding sponsorship from various audiences, using specific tools and methods.

## Vision Understood and Implemented

Research by Peter Morris (2005) in the United Kingdom centers around "evidence that the front end of projects is where things can go badly wrong and, conversely, where there is the best chance of positively influencing the chances of a successful outcome." Morris argues that "projects are only done for a reason—generally the sponsor's reason—often, though not always, expressible in financial terms" and that "following the *PMBOK Guide* elements may be sufficient to deliver projects properly in process and practice terms but probably is not enough to ensure that the project is successful. . . . To do the latter, one needs to concentrate more on managing the front end." And "managing the interaction between the project and its environment to best meet project requirements is as critical as simply building the project to some set of approved requirements. . . . Managing the front-end definition is as much a part of the domain as managing execution."

While it is important to communicate achieved results to interested stakeholders once the project is complete, it is also key to communicate throughout the project between the project manager and the project sponsor, giving feedback among them. Feedback throughout the project ensures that information is flowing so that changes or adjustments can be made to achieve project success.

A graduate course required a case study to be submitted every week. A grade was given, no comments were provided, and no discussion occurred in the classroom. Over the duration of the course, little noticeable improvement occurred in quality of the cases submitted or grades received. In another course, the instructor read sample comments from each case after the first submittal. Numerous comments appeared on the cases handed back to the students each week. Both the quality of submittals and grades received made remarkable improvement during the course.

This lesson made an indelible impact on me (Englund) about the power of feedback. Every project manager (and project sponsor) has this tool available—it is simply a matter of deciding to use it. Career development occurs when people get feedback on what they do well as well as receive suggestions for how to do things better. This tool is so powerful that it can even dwarf or minimize the need to point out what people do wrong. By reinforcing strengths, weaknesses fall by the wayside.

High-performing teams are ones who regularly submit their work to each other in order to improve it. They are less competitive and more collaborative. No one is expected to get the work right the first time and on one's own. Excellent results come from peer reviews, driven by a shared value of accountability for the success of the team, project, or organization.

Unfortunately, many people feel compelled to correct the failings of others. Instead, there is greater potential to excel and achieve better results when people invoke the feedback tool to reinforce positive efforts.

Why do people play games for hours or work so hard for a competitive event? Because they get a score. This feedback is a motivating factor. Why not use the same approach in project management?

Given that most professionals have some discretionary control over what they work on or where they spend their time and that they probably have multiple projects to work on, how can sponsors get stakeholders to give top priority to their projects? This question has multiple answers, and in practice, most people are well served by asking the question every day throughout their careers and in finding unique answers for each individual they need to work with.

While there is no one right answer, a best practice answer is to provide feedback. In an environment where feedback is scarce, a person who regularly and promptly provides constructive responses stands out. Early feedback that corrects the use of a repetitive methodology is always welcomed because it saves on rework. Suggestions to revise the order of material presented are wonderful because these represent easy corrections that immensely improve value. A person who takes the time to provide this feedback may be treasured as a rare commodity.

Other feedback may be comments on a report or paper, questions that prompt additional forms of inquiry, statements about what works well or invokes interest and could be expanded, pointing out areas of work that are unclear, and enthusiastic support for a course of action. Make it a high priority to respond to every inquiry, share what thinking processes are going on, develop and use consistent criteria for decision making, communicate all news whether good or bad, provide reflective answers to questions, tame anxiety responses and provide space for others to come through, and generally become known for quality responses. Appreciate the ebb and flow of team dynamics—using discretion about when to push and when to let a natural energy drive the process. These steps demonstrate that the leader is paying attention to the people responsible for success.

The case for feedback hinges on establishing shared values and putting them into practice. The results will be extraordinary. Early in each project, take the time to emphasize the importance of each person's contribution. Make explicit commitments to be accountable for overall success and to extract the optimum contribution from each other. Demonstrate these values profusely every day, both by soliciting feedback from and providing it to others.

Feedback is one of those important issues that can generate major problems. Because the results of a solution can be closely linked to the political issues in an organization, feedback can upset some individuals while pleasing others. The timing and content of feedback needs to be consistent with past practices. Speaking the truth should be the norm, even if the results being spoken are not positive. We strongly recommend repeating this feedback periodically, because reactions and behaviors from various project stakeholders are different.

It is also important for the customer or client organization to recognize the interests of the provider to make a profit and stay in business—creating a win-win relationship. Chief information officers (CIOs) and others who manage vendors, suppliers, and contractors may be tempted to push so hard for a great deal that they drive their suppliers away or out of business. This does not serve the client organization well. A preferred approach is to treat these suppliers as partners; communicate openly, especially about other suppliers, so that a genuine competition ensues; and give them feedback that will help them do a better job of serving you.

Practice three-way communication as a practical means to ensure that feedback is effective. The first way is speaking a message. The second way is the receiver stating that the message was heard and understood. The third way is the initial sender verifying that the message was understood and a desired action will be taken. In the movie *Jerry Maguire*, when sports agent Jerry wants to retain athlete Rod, Rod says, "I hear that you hear what I said but do you hear what I said—*show me the money.*" Jerry has to scream back those words before Rod will accept Jerry as his agent. By the end of the conversation, the vision is not only stated but fully understood.

In some projects, feedback data are periodically collected and quickly communicated to different stakeholders. Table 7.1 shows a feedback action plan designed to provide information to sponsors using different media.

### Table 7.1 Feedback Action Plan

| Data Collected | Time | Media | Timing of Feedback | Action Required |
|---|---|---|---|---|
| 1. Previous project survey | Beginning of the project | Meeting, survey summary | Kick-off meeting, planned meeting | Adjust actions or approach |
| 2. Project implementation survey | Beginning of the implementation | Survey | | Adjust approach |
| 3. Interviews or approach | One month later | Meeting | Meeting date | Adjust actions |
| 4. Project implementation feedback or survey | End of implementation | Survey | Project implementation review | Adjust actions or approach |

Feedback data are collected during the project at four specific time intervals and communicated back to the sponsor. To provide feedback and manage this feedback process, consider the following steps:

1. *Be quick.* Be as quick as possible communicating. It does not matter if it is good or bad news; it is important to let sponsors and stakeholders involved in the project have the information as soon as possible.

2. *Simplify.* Be simple communicating the data. Be concise, condensing the important data you have because the most important thing is how to learn through the feedback provided and make the best decisions possible in the moment.

3. *Explore.* Find out the role of the project manager and project sponsor in the feedback situation. Sometimes borders are invaded, and that generates conflicts.

4. *Use.* Use negative data in a constructive way and use positive data in a cautious way. Always be positive; if other people can learn, you can learn too.

5. *Select.* Select the language of the meeting and communication very carefully. Take into account the organizational environment because it makes a big difference.

6. *Ask.* Ask the other person for reaction to the data and for recommendations. Remind the person to be focused on what happened, not who was the good guy or bad guy in each situation.

7. *Respect.* Respect each other. Be supportive or confrontational as the situation requires, while always seeking dialogue.

8. *React.* React and act on the data. Lessons learned prepare us to take action.

9. *Secure.* Obtain agreement from all key project stakeholders.

10. *Be short.* Keep the feedback process short and concise.

People give feedback to others based on their perceptions of the reality and the experiences they lived before. Many are familiar with different perceptions of six blind men about an elephant. The poem "The Blind Man and the Elephant" by John Godfrey Saxe is based on an ancient Hindu parable.

*It was six men of Indostan*
*To learning much inclined,*
*Who went to see the Elephant—(Though all of them*
          *were blind),*
*That each by observation—Might satisfy his mind.*
*The First approached the Elephant,*
*And happening to fall*
*Against his broad and sturdy side—At once began to bawl:*
*"God bless me! but the Elephant—Is very like a wall!"*
*The Second, feeling of the tusk,*
*Cried, "Ho! what have we here?*
*So very round and smooth and sharp?—To me 'tis mighty clear*
*This wonder of an Elephant—Is very like a spear!"*
*The Third approached the animal,*
*And happening to take*
*The squirming trunk within his hands—Thus boldly*
          *up and spake:*
*"I see," quoth he, "the Elephant—Is very like a snake!"*
*The Fourth reached out an eager hand,*
*And felt about the knee.*
*"What most this wondrous beast is like—Is mighty plain,"*
          *quoth he;*
*"'Tis clear enough the Elephant—Is very like a tree!"*
*The Fifth who chanced to touch the ear,*
*Said: "E'en the blindest man*
*Can tell what this resembles most;—Deny the fact who can,*
*This marvel of an Elephant—Is very like a fan!"*
*The Sixth no sooner had begun*
*About the beast to grope,*
*Than, seizing on the swinging tail—That fell within his scope,*
*"I see," quoth he, "the Elephant—Is very like a rope!*

*And so these men of Indostan*
*Disputed loud and long,*
*Each in his own opinion—Exceeding stiff and strong,*
*Though each was partly in the right—And all were*
*in the wrong!*

The point is not who is right and who is wrong. The value of receiving feedback from different people is so powerful because somebody else can perceive key things that other people can not.

## Structured Feedback to the Customer Sponsor

We strongly recommend giving feedback to the customer sponsor in a structured way. Use a "radar chart" like the one shown to Figure 7.1. Give feedback on each of the aspects in the chart (see Exhibit 7.1). Use a scale from 0 (poor) to 10 (excellent) for each element to be scored.

### Figure 7.1  Feedback "Radar Chart"

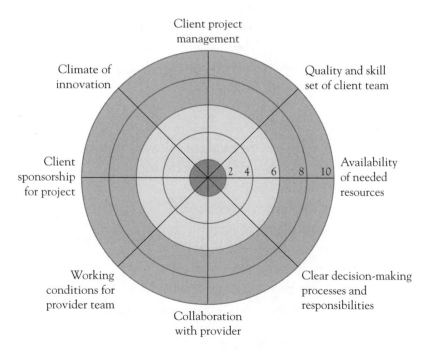

## Exhibit 7.1  Feedback Assessment Tool

Client project management    _____

Quality and skill set of client team    _____

Availability of needed resources    _____

Clear decision-making processes and responsibilities    _____

Collaboration with provider    _____

Working conditions for provider team    _____

Client sponsorship for project    _____

Climate of innovation    _____

# Review of Sponsorship Execution

There are two possibilities and advantages in the process of reviewing sponsorship: For the PM to give a structured feedback to the provider sponsor and for the sponsor to review his or her sponsorship execution. Use the questionnaire in Exhibit 7.2 to focus your feedback.

## Exhibit 7.2  Feedback Questionnaire

To help focus your feedback, answer each question yes or no.

**Questions About the Sponsor**

1. Has the sponsor participated in all key meetings?    Yes    No

2. Has the sponsor communicated proactively and sold the project across the organization to create buy-in and participation?    Yes    No

3. Did the sponsor support the PM and project team in obtaining required resources and budgets?    Yes    No

4. Did the sponsor take time communicating with the PM and project team, provide guidance and coaching, and review key document proposals and presentations?    Yes    No

5. Did the sponsor monitor the project, including financials?    Yes    No

6. Was the sponsor active in escalating situations and involved in solving them?    Yes    No

## Exhibit 7.2  Feedback Questionnaire, Cont'd

7. Did the sponsor show a good understanding of the PM, including support for knowledge sharing?    Yes    No

8. Was the sponsor involved in the organization and cochair in all key project review or steering meetings?    Yes    No

9. Did the sponsor create a relationship with other sponsors and other key upper managers to demonstrate teamwork?    Yes    No

10. Did the sponsor develop a good understanding of business issues and challenges and provide advice and access to best practices?    Yes    No

11. Was the sponsor active in positioning the project within the organization and reducing ambiguity about project priorities?    Yes    No

12. Did the sponsor support the PM and project team in conflict resolutions and escalations?    Yes    No

**Questions About the Project Manager**

13. Did the PM participate in all key meetings?    Yes    No

14. Did the PM communicate proactively with all involved organizations about tasks, ownership, commitment, and project status?    Yes    No

15. Did the PM accurately specify requirements for resources and budgets? Yes    No

16. Did the PM provide real-time information to upper management, avoiding surprises and promoting proactive decision making?    Yes    No

17. Did the PM track the project, including task completion, changes, and financials?    Yes    No

18. Did the PM escalate issues when appropriate and provide all relevant information to resolve conflicts?    Yes    No

19. Did the PM demonstrate a working knowledge of project management and applying best practices?    Yes    No

20. Did the PM facilitate effective core team meetings?    Yes    No

21. Did the PM form productive relationships with counterparts in other areas of the organization?    Yes    No

22. Did the PM develop a good understanding of business issues and challenges and provide advice and access to best practices?    Yes    No

23. Was the PM proactive in considering project outcome life cycle results and new business opportunities?    Yes    No

24. Did the PM achieve the expected results?    Yes    No

## Point of View from Upper Managers

We asked upper managers in international organizations the following questions:

1. Are key practices employed to define, obtain, and sustain a sponsor in your organization?

2. Why is the sponsor role important for you?

3. How should sponsors "walk the walk"?

4. What is the single best contribution to excellence in sponsorship?

Here are some of the answers we received.

### Answers to Question 1

As of today, sponsors are primarily determined by the scope of the project and are more a natural selection rather than based on a thorough analysis. Key factors to decide on the level of the sponsor are investment and business criticality. IT cross-functional, enterprisewide projects with global impact are typically sponsored by a member of the IMT or, in very special cases, by a member of the board of directors. Business projects do fall into biz reps, although this is not always the rule, and for certain projects at certain levels there can be a mix.

—Alvaro Garrido, PGID-Engineering Roche

The project sponsor is the manager who is commercially and financially responsible for the project and its business outcome. The project sponsor is the orderer of the project, the primary risk taker for the project, the one who makes the tollgate decisions. These are based on an assessment of the project's alignment with the organization's business goals. The project sponsor at Ericsson has normally experience from customer projects as project manager, account manager, or member of the Project Steering Group. The project sponsor should be familiar with the tollgate directive and this model.

—Adriano Brilli, RM/TEI Ericsson

## Answers to Question 2

To ensure focus and alignment with business priorities, avoiding deviations as the project or program progresses. Assess changes when required. To secure funds, to assess and manage risk, and to ensure that correct methodology is applied.

—Alvaro Garrido, PGID-Engineering Roche

The purpose of the project sponsor role is to ensure that the manager who is the financial risk taker for the project has defined responsibilities and tasks in the project. The project sponsor is responsible for tollgate assessments being carried out at the appropriate times and for making tollgate decisions. The project sponsor sets the priorities for the project and should provide support in negotiations with resource owners within the Ericsson organization as well as with third-party organizations. The project sponsor will chair the Change Control Board (CCB), where change decisions will be made that will have a greater impact on budget, time, or functionality. Every change request is a possibility to increase the margin. The project sponsor shall support the Core Three team when negotiations regarding change are required with the customer.

—Adriano Brilli, RM/TEI Ericsson

## Answers to Question 3

Participating in the definition of the project governance and sticking to and delivering on the responsibilities assigned to him or her (attending the meetings, adhering to the project methodology guidelines, producing the executive reports,. . . etc.). He or she should seek active participation, provoke discussion, and challenge achievements and deliverables. By establishing controls and providing content-based feedback and direction on a regular basis. By standing before upper management when resources are needed or unexpected problems or deviations pop up.

—Alvaro Garrido, PGID-Engineering Roche

Identifying the business interface to the customer and establishing mutually beneficial relationships with the customer and other relevant stakeholders. It is an additional specific responsibility of the sponsor managing the business agreement with the customer, if applicable. The sponsor must appoint the other members of the project steering group and chair the project steering group meetings. He or she must identify the external and internal receivers of the project outcome.

—Adriano Brilli, RM/TEI Ericsson

## Answer to Question 4

Vision and commitment.

—Alvaro Garrido, PGID-Engineering Roche

## "CEOs Can't Do It Alone," by Payson Hall, Catalysis Group, Inc. (2003)

Most organizations are not facing a data problem as much as "an effective response to data" problem. What is the value of improved portfolio information if we aren't responding effectively to the project-level information already available?

Suppose that accurate status is available for projects, but project team members or managers hesitate to deliver problematic information because they don't want to rock the boat or play the messenger in a "shoot the messenger" scenario. What if meaningful status is reported but never reaches the sponsor through the competing stimuli associated with multiple projects, changing technology, and a dynamic business environment? Worse yet, imagine that sponsors receive news about project problems but are unsure of how to respond. Creating "enterprise dashboard" views of the data will not help an organization address these challenges, but better sponsorship will.

While it may disappoint some of the vendors poised to help you tackle your problems with EPM tools, a prelude to procurement should be an evaluation of your organization's sponsorship skills. If you find your sponsors are receiving and acting effectively on status information at the project level, perhaps your organization would be served by more consolidated views of data. If instead you find that your sponsorship skills need improvement, your resources might be better invested in honing these fundamentals. Most organizations can realize a tangible benefit from improved sponsorship in just a few months. Every organization has a few projects that are ill conceived and unlikely to deliver value. Consider the benefit of being able to cancel projects that represent future disappointments earlier. All of the resource investments not made in the doomed projects move directly to the bottom line. Avoidance of needless expense has a tremendous ROI.

It's not that project management isn't working or isn't necessary, it just isn't sufficient. Project management is about defining, planning, and managing projects, but it is also about supporting timely and effective decision making related to those projects—decision making that occurs not at the project manager's level, but at the level of the sponsor and above. There is a common misconception that we throw tough projects at good project managers and then the desired results are miraculously delivered on time and on budget. In practice, project management is as much about helping sponsors respond effectively when project reality is failing to live up to expectations. For this process to work, there must be a sponsor involved who represents the interests of the organization, is open to receiving information (including bad news), and is willing and able to respond. . . .

From the CIO perspective, a sponsor's timely assessment of project viability and estimated value is essential to sound decision making. Organizational leaders need information about individual projects to manage the contents and priority of the entire portfolio of projects, moving to redefine or cancel those efforts that no longer seem profitable or aligned with organizational goals. CIOs have a huge stake in the quality of sponsorship because they have a huge stake in the quality of the organization's decision making. Before investing in additional tools to present project status data in innovative ways, most organizations would do better to ensure that project sponsors understand their role and have the skill and information needed to perform their vital function in the project management process. If your sponsors don't know how to drive, a new dashboard won't help. If your sponsors don't know they are sponsors, who is driving?

## Summary

The sponsor is in a difficult position between the project team and the client. A key is to find the right balance to perform as project sponsor. Spend more time communicating with the team at the front end of the project and maintain good communication throughout. Receiving feedback from various stakeholders may prove extremely helpful for all concerned.

Even in situations where the client, customer, or end user is unknown, feedback is necessary for all players in order to improve. This chapter makes a strong plea to provide more feedback to others as a daily practice. Its value is immense as a means to improve performance, increase morale, and achieve desired results. Our questionnaires provide a way to focus on and measure how well sponsors and others in the organization provide feedback to each other. Take the time to address these issues.

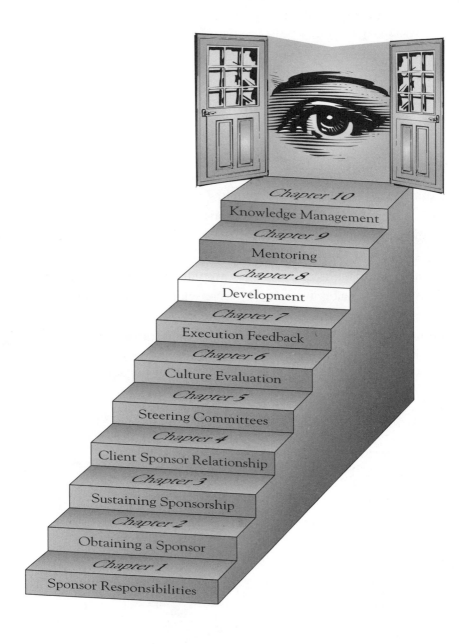

Chapter 10
Knowledge Management

Chapter 9
Mentoring

Chapter 8
Development

Chapter 7
Execution Feedback

Chapter 6
Culture Evaluation

Chapter 5
Steering Committees

Chapter 4
Client Sponsor Relationship

Chapter 3
Sustaining Sponsorship

Chapter 2
Obtaining a Sponsor

Chapter 1
Sponsor Responsibilities

# 8

# SPONSORSHIP DEVELOPMENT

*The wisest mind has something yet to learn.*

*—George Santayana*

Getting good support for project management in an organization, especially from upper management, is a key for sustainable project success. To be able, as a manager, to address all issues regarding the project world is not easy, and good sponsors do not appear by accident. Managers also need training, experience, and practice.

Some managers have not lived on the customer site and never managed a customer project. They may not understand how a project manager feels and the importance of project planning. Upper managers appear to believe that project managers are like magicians, solving every issue, no matter what type, with a magic wand. They often do not put effort into developing and maintaining strong relationships with customer upper-level counterparts, helping them make good business decisions, and supporting project manager work and efforts.

This chapter explains how sponsors can develop their skills to contribute to project success. We include a real story about working effectively with upper management sponsors and how that was a key to success. But we encountered many obstacles. This chapter explains how seasoned project management professionals deal with the obstacles and the project management processes to be followed, including selling the concept and developing a training curriculum.

## Background

This story started with the Spanish Project Office creation that arose from the need to relieve project managers of administrative tasks associated with managing a project. The consulting organization believed that the Project Office should help the project manager improve efficiency, facilitate getting the right tools, and align services with the needs of the project environment.

At the beginning of the project, I (Bucero) ran a survey to determine how well the Hewlett-Packard Consulting (HPC) organization supported project management. Sixty-five percent of the people answered the survey. The results cited no holistic view of the project portfolio, lack of knowledge (reuse culture), no consistent approach for complex projects, poor scope management, bad risk identification, lack of sponsorship, and project closing delays.

One key area chosen for improvement was the lack of sponsorship. Knowing that people who have never worked on a project have difficulty understanding how to achieve project success, the organization wanted to increase support provided by its sponsor to the project managers.

The key to getting upper management support at this point was showing how the PMO solved current problems and how it could have an immense business impact. A complete business case was presented to the management team in the language and format of "management speak."

The HPC Project Office stakeholders were the managers of the business and solutions that influence both end users and upper managers alike. Through a stakeholder analysis, I could determine how different individuals influence decisions throughout the project. This kind of analysis helped me understand the levels of concern and authority of the management team.

That means better understanding the different levels of project culture within the management team and how those behaviors or patterns influence the delivery of results by project managers. It turns out that one of the most important contributions of the PMO was sponsorship development. Sponsorship is a commitment by the upper management and leaders to support and be involved in major projects and initiatives from the start to the end. It is important that the project sponsor and project manager meet regularly and frequently (after every team meeting is wise) to review both teamwork and team task issues. This interaction between the project manager and the project sponsor is fundamental. Using e-mail as the only method for communicating team status is not enough. The personal interaction allows the project sponsor to judge what is going on and sense issues to be raised. In this way, the project sponsor facilitates problem solving more quickly, and emerging problems are identified and addressed early.

I was able to demonstrate that although the project sponsor was not an active member of the team, the person in that position was a resource that served as motivator and barrier buster. Communication is key. I suggested that the management team define a clear agreement on how to interact, communicate, and ensure progress.

## Obstacles and Issues

"Go ahead, and move fast!" That demand is a real and recurring business situation. When I tried to demonstrate to my management team that all projects must be defined and planned to be well executed and implemented, they threw up many obstacles. Comments like "Please don't create more overhead" and "Just do it" were common. But the real problems were the weak project culture, the lack of training, and the short-term mentality exhibited by upper managers.

Managers had little time, before presenting a proposal, to review project scope, time, and risk with the project manager and the team. "What we know" about the project (customer, end user) and "what we don't know" were distinctions that eluded us. It is initially easy to push on but difficult in practice. Short-term business orientation is not compatible with a project-oriented business approach. Projects need time to be planned and implemented; they need project managers who have been trained, mentored, and coached; and most important, they need to be sponsored and supported by the delivery organization.

PMO quality reviews helped us discover some issues, lack of knowledge, and bad practices, but when business results are on target, the management team does not give much priority to these issues. The sentence "If it works, don't change it" was often repeated. But good short-term results may not be good results over the long term, and things eventually did start to go downhill. When bad results appeared, I used them to convince the management team about the importance of a culture of mentoring, coaching, and sponsorship. That was when I suggested that the management team be trained in sponsorship. Slowly, they came to believe that to have an adequate interface between the service provider and the customer is fundamental for project success. Important projects must be linked to the company strategy and need to have upper-level management support.

People who are stressed by organizational targets and objectives are less eager to collaborate and be supportive. I had many face-to-face meetings at different management levels in the organization, but I was not successful in the beginning. Persistence and discipline imposed from above were keys for project success.

Another management trend I observed was that the project sponsor came too close to the team and sometimes interfered, dominated, or manipulated. The project sponsor role is a challenging and sometimes awkward job, but the project sponsor must not substitute for the project manager. It is not appropriate to ignore or tolerate such behavior. These situations call for tact and diplomacy on the part of the program manager to manage upward.

## Direct Efforts to Improve Organizational Culture

We developed a plan, including issues like these:

- Find projects that have a positive bottom-line impact on the corporation.

- Use proven project management principles.
- Determine and nurture individuals who already support project management.
- Learn to thrive in a political environment.
- Become comfortable communicating with senior executives.

The main improvements focused on two areas: first, that people use the PMO's services, and second, that all members of the management team be trained in sponsorship. Initially, some managers refused because they believed that they were performing well and acting in the right way as sponsors. The turning point came when the senior manager asked the management team to attend management meetings and participate in the training sessions.

The sponsorship training focused on the following topics:

- The fact that every project needs a sponsor and that sponsorship is especially crucial and essential in complex and large projects
- That project sponsors should be members of the local management team, empowered by all businesses, assigned for the full project life cycle, and invest between 10 to 20 percent of their time in working with the project team and client
- Defining key responsibilities
- Establishing measures for the project sponsor
- Understanding and positioning client cultures
- Recognizing that sponsorship is a question of mind-set, commitment, and competence

Excellence in sponsorship has a direct impact on project financial performance. A sponsorship culture helps continue existing business and also generate new business. Five elements guide a technology implementation and change effort:

- *Identifying stakeholders:* Running a stakeholder analysis and identifying who is who in the organization. Qualify the degree of concern and authority of every stakeholder.

- *Selecting stakeholders:* Making a decision about which stakeholders can be assigned as sponsors, focusing on degree of authority, belief in the organization, and desire to perform that role.
- *Coaching stakeholders in sponsorship:* Training stakeholders selected as sponsors and clarifying roles and responsibilities during the whole project life cycle. Clearly define all measures for success. Identify owners in the company or organization.
- *Mentoring stakeholders:* To measure results during sponsorship implementation, monitoring deviations and taking agreements on action plans, defining dates and owners for each action item. Establish metrics that allow room for improvement and recognize the efforts and achievement of people involved.
- *Executing action plans:* To start up all action plans assigning the needed resources and using upper management support. The responsibility of each action plan is from the owner assigned. One of the problems found during the training sessions was that after people are assigned as owners for action items, nothing happens. Distributing meeting results or minutes as soon as possible, following up each action with the owner after the meeting, and talking with my upper manager after those sessions to review the action plan were extremely helpful. After training sessions, I persuaded upper managers to communicate, as a must, that every project in the organization larger than $1 million should have a sponsor assigned for the whole project life cycle. That process was implemented, and sponsors have been learning through the practice. At the end of those types of projects, we run a retrospective analysis to find out what went well and what did not go as well, what we learned, and what needs to be changed for the future. Retrospective analysis was positive and is strongly recommended for every organization that needs to manage a project portfolio effectively.

## The Importance of the PMO

This organization improved its effectiveness and efficiency because it had a small but dedicated group of professionals to focus on the project management process. The project office started by addressing the most pressing needs of the organization and expanded its role with each success. It attacked the pervasive issue of weak sponsorship by getting the attention of upper managers to realize how their role could be improved. It then trained them in basic concepts and behaviors that make a big difference. Personal communications were extensive and mandatory factors for achieving new behaviors. Through this means, the project office can forge the path for the organization to replicate its successes. It ensures that a solid base of best practices is in place for continued growth into the future. Project managers obtain the training and support they need to deliver results to customers. People in the project office become increasingly valuable as skilled change agents. The journey toward excellence is continuous, driven by the PMO.

## Best Practices

- People who have never worked on a project have difficulty understanding that to achieve project success, the organization must support the project manager.

- The key to getting upper management support was showing how the PMO solved current problems and provided immense business impact. A complete business case was presented to the management team in the language and format of "management speak."

- Sponsorship is a commitment by upper management and leaders to support and be involved in major projects and initiatives from the start to the end.

- Personal interaction allows the project sponsor to judge what is going on and sense issues to be raised. In this way, the project sponsor facilitates problem solving more quickly, and emerging problems are identified and addressed early.

- Excellence in sponsorship affects project financial performance. Developing a sponsorship culture helps meet current business commitments and increase capability for the organization to generate new business.

## Recommendations

Executives need to know what project management means and that well-managed projects have a big business impact. Organize sessions for executives; help them get the training they need. Start with short sessions (two to three hours long), and create project management awareness.

Speak the language that management understands. Assess the environment, and be conscious of other patterns and values in the organization. Define a glossary of PM terms for managers. This takes time but is very productive. Successful organizations are able to speak a common language, but some parts of the organization may still may need to use a dictionary at times.

Show and explain to executives that the sponsor role starts at the beginning and goes to the end of every project. The sponsor may be the "bodyguard" for the project manager.

Promote dialogue and communication between project managers and executives. Executives can learn more about daily project activities to keep them in alignment with strategic goals and be able to do more to benefit each project, as well as benefit the organization.

Executives may need to be "snoopy" in looking out for their customers. Be conscious about their problems, needs, and requirements. Invite executives to customer meetings. Facilitate the communication process in the organization.

## Selling Process

Effective sellers are ones who are convinced and knowledgeable about the product they sell. To sell the need of sponsorship training, know the answers to the following questions:

How many projects do you have in your organization?

What are your organizational priorities?

What are your project results, time, budget, schedule, and risk?

What is your organizational culture?

What is your management culture?

Do you think your communication process could be improved?

Who are your customers?

Taking those matters into account brings an assessment regarding the organizational environment. Capture data that identify the need represented by the current situation. Show executives the advantages of a more desirable future state where key people are trained in sponsorship. Here are additional questions to ask:

How many projects are you sponsoring?

What is the status of those projects?

Have you visited the project customer, client, or end user in the last month?

Questions such as those can reveal, for example, that some sponsors are expected to sponsor "too many projects," that some sponsors believe that knowing project status is only the project manager's responsibility, and that many sponsors do not meet with their project customers regularly.

In that case, some of the advantages for executives being trained as sponsors would be to know more about the projects they sponsor; to know their customers better, gaining more credibility; and to give more support to their project managers.

All of this converges to generate more business, to offer better service and results to customers, and to be more credible. That takes time, dedication, and training. To dedicate one full morning, as an executive, to be trained in sponsorship is to develop the right executive skills for the twenty-first century. Sell the idea to executives that knowing more will get more in return. What you know and what you don't know about your projects and customers can hurt or help, depending on how you use that information.

Are you measured by customer satisfaction? If the answer is yes, listen to the PM lead in your organization. Let this person explain to you what is expected from the sponsor.

## Approval Process

Being responsible for the PMO in a multinational organization that delivered external customer projects, I (Bucero) spent almost six months attending monthly management meetings and showing a big list of delayed and poorly managed projects because of a lack of PM experience, big risk, and lack of management support. The slot of time I had for my presentation was always ten minutes. Most of the meeting action plans consisted of talking to project managers to correct deviations from plan. I insisted that the main problem was not the project managers. Management had to change some behaviors and gain skills to improve the organization's projects and overall effectiveness.

The sixth month, I was lucky. The organizational results were bad, and the management team looked for someone in the organization to blame. I offered to demonstrate that most of the executives in the organization could change their behaviors. I could arrange a workshop with a trainer from Germany. My managing director said yes. As is far too common in many situations, management wake-up calls come only when someone from another organization can come in and preach the same things you have been preaching, but in another language.

The lesson learned was not to focus on site solutions but to consider using resources outside the organization. Sometimes words said by other colleagues or in another language act as magic wands.

## Action Plan

We decided to focus our sponsorship training on the follow points:

- Project sponsor responsibilities
- Sustaining sponsorship checklist
- Client sponsor relationship template
- Planning and executing steering committees
- Client sponsorship and culture evaluation

- Client feedback "radar chart"
- Sponsorship execution feedback

The training session was set up and was well attended. Benefits were achieved and are ongoing. Many of the lessons learned form the basis for this book.

## Case Study: Creative Leadership Decision, by Kimberly Liegel, Liegel Enterprises LLC (2005)

In the midst of implementing a PMO at a software company, where I worked as director of program management, one of the biggest challenges was the overall cultural change necessary for the adoption of the project management practices that engineers recognized we needed but nonetheless scorned.

With only influential authority, I would need support from the top down in driving organizational change. To implement anything successfully across the multiple functional disciplines within our organization, it was going to take collaborative leadership with my peers—engineering directors more specifically—to drive and internalize this down to the "hands-on-keyboards" level.

To achieve this, I fostered a two-pronged collaborative leadership initiative. This included a special invitation event across all functional disciplines with the company's most respected, top-quality software engineers, quality assurance analysts, product managers, and project managers. We ran this as a direct-level, cross-organizational team initiative to create an environment that recognized and rewarded leadership and best-practices sharing.

This event created a groundswell of understanding and commitment to implementing many of the project management processes I was struggling to get others to accept.

The second prong was to initiate a parallel director-level team project to develop and implement a standard software development life cycle with all the supporting processes, templates, and defined roles and responsibilities. Once the directors' feet were to the fire, exposed and held close by the people that attended the leadership event, real collaboration and ownership happened.

## Summary

It is naive to expect excellent sponsorship practices to happen by accident or wishful thinking. It takes a wake-up call and a selling process to help sponsors understand both the potential and the responsibilities of the sponsorship role. Commit to carry this message across the organization, and set up training that helps sponsors develop awareness and skills as well as network with other sponsors to share best practices. The outline for sponsorship training and case studies about implementing sponsorship training in this chapter can be particularly useful.

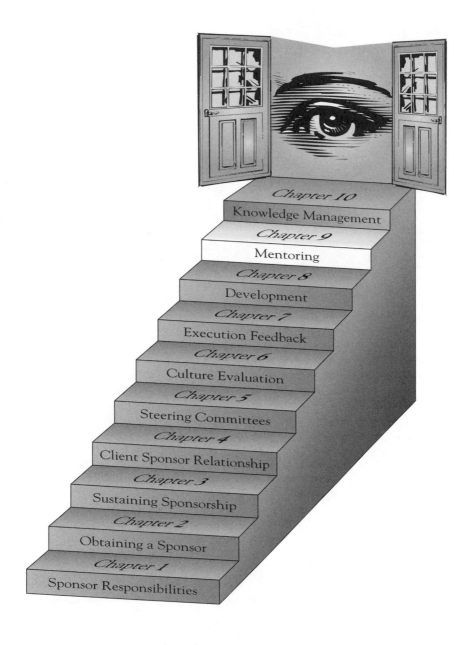

Chapter 10
Knowledge Management

Chapter 9
Mentoring

Chapter 8
Development

Chapter 7
Execution Feedback

Chapter 6
Culture Evaluation

Chapter 5
Steering Committees

Chapter 4
Client Sponsor Relationship

Chapter 3
Sustaining Sponsorship

Chapter 2
Obtaining a Sponsor

Chapter 1
Sponsor Responsibilities

# 9

# SPONSORSHIP
# MENTORING

Never discourage anyone who continually makes
progress, no matter how slow.

—*Plato*

Mentoring means two people collaborating for career development, defining career goals and professional development goals. It is an interactive journey and also a mutually accountable relationship. Mentoring is not counseling family, work performance, or personal conflicts. It is not tutoring or teaching, it is not a way to get a job reference, it is not counseling in getting a new job, and it is not a constant "gripe" session.

This chapter highlights the contribution of mentoring to excellence in sponsorship. We describe benefits to both sides of the party and to the organization. An example demonstrates an enhanced view of sponsorship that includes speaking truth to power and involves the mentoring process.

When talking about mentoring executives, we mean people who are usually very busy, so we need to sell them on the benefits regarding that activity. We can find benefits for mentees and also for mentors.

Some benefits for mentees are faster career growth, faster growth in business, better organizational and project success, and recognition and feeling of achievement.

Some benefits for mentors are a way to "give back," a chance to sharpen one's leadership skills, an opportunity to be the trusted adviser of another person for organizational and business success, and sharing lessons learned as a way of helping others.

## What Is Mentoring?

Mentoring is a way of integrating the mentee into the organization; a system for learning organizational and project rules, norms, and guidelines; a confidential relationship; an opportunity for the mentor to share professional and personal experiences; and an opportunity for the mentee to receive advice and direction.

Mentoring is not a path to promotion, a forum for recognition, a way around any manager, or a program designed to involve the mentor in performance problems.

## What Is a Mentor?

A mentor is a confidential adviser who offers support and encourages people. A mentor is a guide who introduces the person in the organization and helps the person to discover the key people and show how the organization works. A mentor is a model who establishes the example of sponsorship practice in the organization and its manner of operation. The mission of a mentor is to help the mentee detect concrete skills to improve and give advice about how to develop them, facilitating the mentee's professional success.

## The Mentor Role

The mentor role is to contribute to the professional and personal development of the mentee. This implies a big responsibility because it is not always easy. The mentee retains responsibility of the leadership in his or her career development for which only he or she is responsible. The mentor can, however, help the mentee identify individual values, clarify expectations, discover strengths and weaknesses, identify opportunities, and become integrated in the organizational environment.

It is fundamental for the mentee to know what is valuable to learn and what the objectives to be achieved are. By clarifying these up front, mentor and mentee can work together on the path to follow. The mentor needs to give honest feedback to the mentee and open the mentee's eyes to real possibilities in the organization. The mentor can share thought processes leading to decisions made that improve overall judgment capabilities.

## Some Clues

Here are some suggestions to help achieve better results through the interaction:

- Listen to the other person. Use ears and mouth the same percentage of the time.
- Respect the person's opinions. It does not matter if they are correct or incorrect. Help the person reach personal conclusions.
- Give objective information, and do not evaluate the other person. Avoid defensive reactions.
- Ask questions. Propose solutions. Give feedback to ensure mutual understanding. Share experiences. Explore different options when a decision must be made.
- Encourage decisions. It is a way of motivation that normally enriches the relationship.
- Provide emotional support when needed.
- If you do not know the answer to a question, say, "I do not know." Look for an answer, but recognize that you are human and cannot have an answer for everything.

## Things That Are Not Helpful

Here is some advice regarding things that are not helpful and are to be avoided.

- Do *not* give unconstructive criticism.
- Do *not* offer to sponsor the mentee in his or her professional career.
- Do *not* try to protect the mentee.
- Do *not* do or say anything that contradicts the mentee's manager.
- Do *not* make decisions for the mentee. Discuss options and their advantages and disadvantages, but allow the decisions to be made by the mentee.

## Facilitating Discussion

Open discussions are stimulating and among the best tools that can be used. Here are suggestions for each mentoring session.

- Clarify problems: ask questions, summarize and paraphrase questions and answers
- Guide discussion: redirect the discussion by asking new questions, ask "What if. . ." questions, help organize subjects, and take notes
- Advocate: involve the mentee, ask for common sense analyses, and look for assumptions
- Explain: recount your experiences, present conceptual models, and talk in general
- Close: review all the things discussed, replan all dilemmas, agree on actions and objectives, and make an appointment for the next meeting

## Difficulties and Suggestions

Sometimes things do not go as well as desired. Table 9.1 lists some difficulties that may be encountered and suggested actions to overcome them.

**Table 9.1  Problems in the Mentoring Relationship**

| *Problem* | *Solution* |
| --- | --- |
| Lack of empathy | Analyze the causes. If you can not deal with them, look for another mentor. |
| Lack of time | Any moment is good: having lunch, at the airport, early in the morning, late in the evening. Reset your priorities. |
| Unrealistic or unachieved expectations | Review expectations periodically. |
| Lack of short-term results | Work on solidifying the relationship. Detecting problems and analyzing them leads to progress. Be persistent and patient. |

## Critical Success Factors

To achieve a successful relationship with a mentee, the mentor must clearly understand the mentor role, make time for mentoring, be inquisitive, and reinforce the mentee's positive behaviors.

## The Mentoring Process

At the start of the mentoring relationship, the initiative comes not from the mentor but from the mentee. However, the mentor can begin thinking about how to help the person even before the first meeting.

Some things to think about in advance might be the duration of the mentoring process, your availability for mentoring, a meeting schedule you might set up right from the start, and the subjects you consider interesting that you would like to cover with the mentee.

The main objective of the mentoring relationship is for the mentor to contribute to the mentee's development. Be as concrete as possible in setting personal objectives and crafting a customized action plan.

Specific details will be different in every relationship, but the following are fairly standard matters for discussion:

- Introduce yourselves to each other.
- Set out expectations for the mentoring process.
- Examine personal and professional expectations and determine if they are realistic.
- Identify and talk about the mentee's strengths and weaknesses.
- Discuss the organizational culture and projects.
- Discuss the mentee's job.
- Examine opportunities for the mentee to move forward.
- Discuss obstacles and how to overcome them.
- Establish a contacts network.

The benefits derived from mentoring are usually more indirect than measurable. It is a practice that creates an environment for successful projects in an organic way—it empowers people to get advice or find answers anywhere inside or outside the organization. It supports innovation through a free flow of information. It is a morale boost for people to know that they are not alone in their struggles and to find a helping hand. Since sponsorship in most organizations does not yet qualify as a core competence, encourage mentoring by those who demonstrate proficiency in sponsorship as a ready means to share the wealth. Mentoring does not take the place of formal training, but it certainly helps. Achieving a mentorship culture establishes that collaboration is more valuable than competition among management ranks.

## Case Study

This case study illustrates the process of speaking truth to power by telling a story. Sponsors are more effective when they apply this process with senior managers; they are also wise to share the process with mentees. The hero of the story served both to demonstrate the precepts in action and to coach others. Start at the top of Figure 9.1 and move clockwise.

# Figure 9.1  A Mentoring Process for Speaking Truth to Power

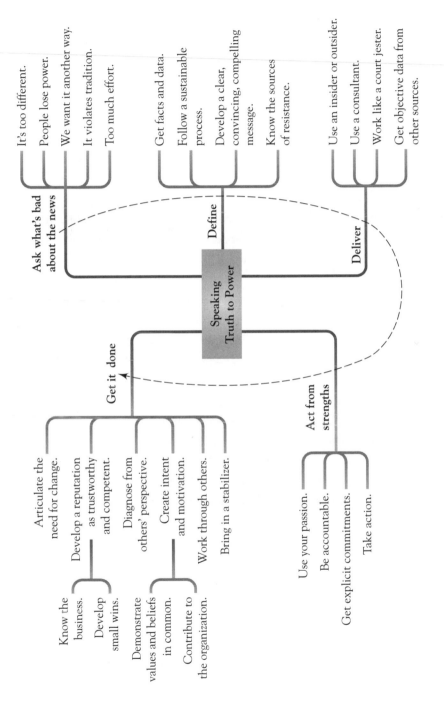

Speaking Truth to Power

**Define**
- Ask what's bad about the news
  - It's too different.
  - People lose power.
  - We want it another way.
  - It violates tradition.
  - Too much effort.
- Get facts and data.
- Follow a sustainable process.
- Develop a clear, convincing, compelling message.
- Know the sources of resistance.

**Deliver**
- Use an insider or outsider.
- Use a consultant.
- Work like a court jester.
- Get objective data from other sources.

**Get it done**
- Articulate the need for change.
  - Know the business.
  - Develop small wins.
- Develop a reputation as trustworthy and competent.
- Diagnose from others' perspective.
  - Demonstrate values and beliefs in common.
  - Contribute to the organization.
- Create intent and motivation.
- Work through others.
- Bring in a stabilizer.

**Act from strengths**
- Use your passion.
- Be accountable.
- Get explicit commitments.
- Take action.

Toni, a project manager at a high-tech company, sensed a big problem. There was no process in place to manage hundreds of technical issues that had been identified within the newly developed computer architecture. Products were now being developed based on this architecture. She knew that the news was bad and getting worse, but she had no more authority than anyone else. However, there was something different about Toni—she was willing to speak truth to power. The complexity of the situation was different from anything else this organization had experienced before, and no one person was directly in charge. No one put in the effort to correct what looked like a massive program.

Toni took the initiative to define the truth. These issues reflected big gaps, errors, or undefined paths in the new computer architecture, issues so significant that new product development was being delayed. If the issues were not resolved rationally, immediate decisions would have to be made that might compromise or severely limit future options. Several product lines would be built on this platform. Architects argued for the purity and integrity of the architecture. Implementers wanted pragmatic solutions that leveraged the work completed to date. Toni was one among dozens of project managers who were depending on the new architecture. She created a compelling picture of why action was required, what needed to be done, how to resolve the issues, and what the results would be. She identified the functional managers whose business was affected by the issues and asked them to get together for a discussion. These upper managers were clearly frustrated by the issues and concerned about getting their projects completed on time. They had no spare resources to resolve issues that they believed other people should be working on.

To deliver the truth, Toni put together a presentation that clearly stated the nature of the issues and their impact on the businesses. She proposed that each business ante up key engineers to meet in study groups that would research the options and propose solutions. People in all project areas needed to review the proposals and agree to adopt them. This work would have to take place concurrently with development efforts already under way. Although not actually required in this case, many times it takes bringing in a trusted outsider, such as somebody in another organization who solved a similar problem or a consultant, to convince people that action is required.

Toni's actions were driven by exercising personal strengths. Her passion and belief in a future state provided courage and energy to take action on this difficult task. Through words and actions, she made it clear that her sole motivation was accountability for success of the program. She asked for their support. Her thorough plan, reinforced by inputs from other people around the organization from whom she sought ideas and backing, convinced this council of upper managers to get on board as a guiding coalition. They asked Toni to sponsor the new program. The upper managers agreed to serve on a steering committee or council. They would prioritize issues, define constraints, ensure that resources were assigned, and follow through on escalated issues.

To get the job done, Toni pointed out the pain that could be felt by each person. She had the ability to design a process that could lead to changes, and she linked the pain and change efforts to the needs of the businesses. By reflecting and drawing on previous experience, she articulated the current reality and defined the steps needed for the change. Fortunately, she had completed a number of prior projects quite successfully. She was technically competent and could understand the difficult nature of the problems being encountered. Her carefully chosen words addressed different perspectives; that is, she addressed the broad picture with upper managers and technical issues with engineers. She consistently demonstrated the values, beliefs, and contributions that this effort would bring to the organization.

Believing in the program, Toni agreed to get it going. She became the leader, the sponsor, the guiding vision, and the workhorse. She also planned to go out of business as a revolutionary. She went to the program management department and requested a project manager. I (Englund) came on board and gradually took over to coordinate the massive cross-organizational efforts. My initial conversation with her revealed many negative expressions, but I somehow had a sense to persevere and later came to realize the negativity came only out of frustration. After we successfully completed the tumultuous first phase, she guided us through the retrospective analysis, continued sponsoring phased efforts, saw that we were on the right path, went back to managing her program full time, and got promoted.

We became quite competent in the new process and alleviated much management anxiety. Resolving these architectural issues was at the heart of the huge success enjoyed by the company. Toni continued taking on new development efforts within the company. Management supported a celebration for the achievements of many that was initiated by the power of one. The group general manager personally signed letters of appreciation for each participant and manager.

Later I sought out Toni as a mentor, as I had been so impressed by her abilities in getting things done in a complex organization. I wanted to know how she did it. One question was how to improve judgment. She suggested observing judgmental situations—make my own call as difficult decisions come up and observe how those in power make the same call. Compare their actions with mine as a way to learn to make better decisions from the masters. Seek to understand their thought processes; probe into the reasons they act as they do. Her feedback on this and other topics was especially valuable and enduring. Later, on a different job, I was able to reciprocate and provide Toni with advice on a project submittal.

## Summary

Sponsors may serve as mentors to project managers and other less experienced sponsors. Sponsors may also want to elicit mentoring advice from others. This chapter points out possible benefits, expectations, and roles. Mentoring is a voluntary process intended to informally aid in achieving excellence in sponsorship through the sharing of thoughts and experiences. The sponsorship process includes working together as a steering committee to receive the truth from those skilled in speaking truth to power; it also includes coaching others on how to speak the truth skillfully and avoid being the messenger of bad news who gets shot.

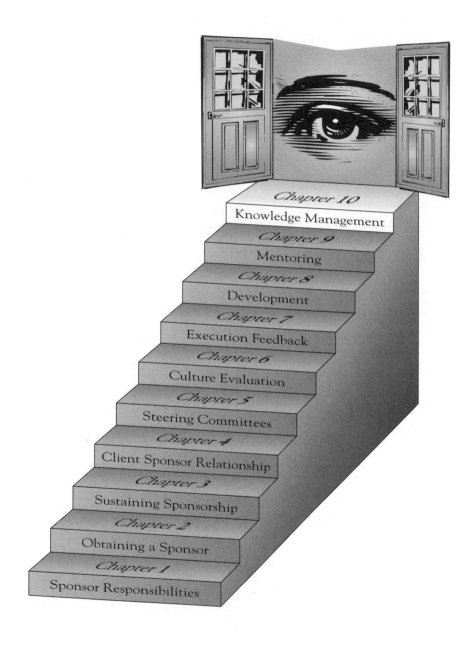

# 10

# KNOWLEDGE MANAGEMENT

If an idea's worth having once, it's worth having twice.
—*Tom Stoppard*

Many managers and project managers—and ultimately the organizations that depend on them—lose the opportunity to learn from their projects because they do not take the time to analyze past results during the project life cycle. Leading with power is an ultimate goal that is enabled by knowledge.

This chapter addresses a sponsor's role in developing a learning organization. The process starts with doing project reviews and taking action on the findings. It also requires developing the means to be effective in a political environment. We present a process to develop a political plan and offer a sample template to record observations and proposed action steps.

## Project Reviews

I (Bucero) have spent more than twenty years in the project business and have always found project managers, from different countries in Europe, living the same experience—lack of time to stop, analyze, and learn from past experiences during the project life cycle. And that learning comes from mistakes as well as from successes.

Some years ago, I was working for a multinational company that sold customer IT projects. I had the responsibility to define and implement a knowledge management process for my consulting organization. We had junior and senior project managers being supported by our project office, but all of them said, "We are reinventing the wheel for every new project, and we never have the opportunity to spend time talking among the team about our projects." It was a crazy situation, but that was the reality. Learning from past experiences is simply not a priority in many organizations. In the solution-selling business, upper managers want to sell more and more, but learning from projects they sponsor does not seem to matter for them.

As a solution-selling organization, we had to achieve profitable results from customer projects. At that time, project results were not very good. On the other hand, the strategic direction was to improve and achieve the next maturity level within the consulting organization. I proposed and received a green light from upper managers to start implementing improved processes using a project office. We started by identifying projects in our portfolio and by identifying the skills and experiences of project managers in the organization. Then, as a project office, we delivered a presentation to project managers and sponsors about how to collect useful information during project life cycles, taking into account the organization's time and cost restraints. The result was to implement "project snapshots," half-day sessions whose purpose is to capture lessons learned during a project, preserve knowledge for reuse, and identify opportunities for skill or methodology improvement for all project stakeholders.

The objectives for these sessions are as follows:

- To reflect on successes and lessons learned in project selling and implementation phases
- To focus around key themes such as project and scope management, communication, issue management, problems, and successes
- To leverage successes and learning to more effectively deliver subsequent phases or projects for clients

- To identify tools and best practices that can be shared more broadly

These sessions generate value for the professionals, for the project team, for the project manager, for the project sponsor, and for the rest of the organization.

For professionals, the sessions leverage team members' work and experience through sharing lessons learned, prevent redundant activities by having all team members understand what each person has worked on and is working on. They resolve issues earlier in the project by getting them surfaced and resolved.

For the project team, the sessions leverage learning and successes for ongoing project work and deliver a more consistent implementation by having everyone on the project get better aligned. And the project team and selling team can better understand client perspectives (when clients are involved in the sessions).

For other project teams, the sessions help them reuse existing tools, identify project teams that have completed similar projects, and use their learning to enhance project outcomes and avoid costly mistakes.

For project managers, the sessions help them understand successes and opportunities in delivering and selling particular methodologies and solutions.

For the project sponsor and the rest of the organization, non-value-adding work is eliminated and more attention gets placed on improving customer satisfaction and increasing sales.

We included time in every project plan across the organization dedicated to review sessions. The session itself takes no more than two hours if planned properly, and the PMO and the project manager need two to three hours of session preparation. After the session, they usually spend about one more hour for reporting purposes.

There are four steps in the process: preparing the session, conducting the session, collecting learning, and sharing the lessons learned.

In preparing the session, the PMO works with the project manager to gather background and identify one or two major project areas or subjects to discuss during the session, creates an agenda, and invites session participants. Inputs from the project sponsor with regard to the business perspective also need to be considered at this stage.

In conducting the session, the project manager, using the PMO as a facilitator, reviews the purpose and themes to discuss and sets the ground rules with the group, defining the "project snapshot process."

In collecting learning, the facilitator takes notes of key lessons or material to be submitted, pulling out sufficient details from the participants so that results are reusable. The facilitator probes meeting attendees for what went well, lessons learned, recommendations, and key collateral and intellectual material for reuse. Key lessons from the session are summarized and formed into a presentation.

In sharing the learning, the project manager and selected team members discuss the lessons learned with appropriate parties. The PMO distributes outcomes to teams responsible for any elements used in the project, including solution development teams, and to people development managers.

After the session, the facilitator collects the outcomes in a document or template and reviews it with the project manager and sponsor prior to distributing it to the team or posting on the Web site.

The PMO plays the role of facilitator and reporter in those sessions. The project office helps the project manager through all project snapshot preparation and logistics. At the beginning, I, as an experienced project manager, facilitated the sessions and trained project managers to conduct them. The results were very good; not only did we get better at doing client projects, but we also earned the right and privilege to handle additional business. I got participant comments such as "It was a great opportunity to talk among team members and managers openly" and "To think and discuss what happened rather than who was guilty has been great."

I talked to executives attending those sessions in different multinational organizations, and most of them believe they were productive sessions and very helpful for creating a culture of open communication.

Customer feedback in different countries is always the same. There may be subtle differences in running project snapshots from country to country, due to different cultures and behaviors, but we find no differences regarding session results. To invest in knowledge management is a key for a successful project business.

A sponsor's role is to initiate and act on these findings, both to make corrections in real time and to improve organizational capability to get work done through projects.

I (Englund) had similar but different experiences with project reviews. After an extensive engineering effort to correct the computer architecture, our sponsor authorized an extensive review of the process. We identified a number of improvements to use people's time more effectively on resolving the remaining issues, based on what we learned by accident rather than by intent during the first phase. The result was fewer people required in less time operating more efficiently. Anxiety disappeared. The platform proved hugely successful.

When the company was first to market with a new personal computer system, a project review identified the contribution of program management. The sponsor staffed a program office for subsequent product development efforts to plan and track progress. Subsequent time-to-market efforts provided continued competitive advantage.

A sales organization that was concerned about lack of support from the service area conducted a review and discovered that sales had committed fundamental errors—starting work before the contract was signed. The sponsor took action to reinforce desired behaviors.

A review of a customer-supplier relationship caught the supplier by surprise when asked the question, "What went right with the relationship?" The customer was prepared to focus only on the negative. In formulating a response, it became clear that many good things were happening as well.

A midcourse retrospective on a large cross-organizational time-constrained project revealed low morale due to the pressure from the sponsor to do the project in an unrealistic time frame. People were doing their best, but the commission of "integrity crimes"—promising the project team recognition upon completion of a project milestone and then failing to do so—did not help. The sponsor did not change, and the project took as long as it required.

A review of a cancelled IT client project came too late to realize that the customer expected the vendor to know and implement everything while the vendor expected to learn together on the job and only do preagreed work. Subsequent engagements avoided these misunderstandings.

Review of an internal project management conference revealed much time spent on efforts receiving low evaluation scores from attendees. These activities were eliminated. Redesigns led to larger, more successful conferences accomplished with less effort. Sponsors lessened their involvement until the larger conferences, due to ever-increasing costs, became victims of their own success.

All these stories would have degenerated into political quagmires if not for knowledge management processes and support by wise sponsors.

## Leading with Power

Project management goes beyond techniques to complete projects on time, scope, and budget. Improving organizational performance depends on getting more accomplished through projects. Just what gets accomplished and how comes under the purview of power and politics. Organizations by their nature are political. To be effective, project managers and their sponsors need to become politically sensitive.

Assessing the environment, rethinking attitudes toward power and politics, and developing an effective political plan are foundation steps. These help to address the power structure in an organization, identify critical stakeholder levels of trust and agreement, develop a guiding coalition, and determine areas of focus—actions that can take place in a project office (see Englund, Graham, and Dinsmore, 2003). Drawing causal loops, both vicious and virtuous, helps depict consequences of behaviors.

Instead of lamenting about a failed project, program, or initiative, learn about power and politics so that project success is optimized. Knowledge, wisdom, and courage, combined with action, have the potential to change your approach to project work. The objective for sharing these examples and insights is to help turn potential victim scenarios into win-win political victories.

## Conceptual Base

A common theme for success or failure of any organizational initiative is building a guiding coalition—a bonding of sponsors and influential people who support the project or initiative. This support or its lack represents a powerful force either toward or away from the goal. Gaining support means the difference between success and failure. Moderate success may occur without widespread political support, but continuing long-term business impact requires alignment of power factors within an organization.

Organizations attempting projects across functions, businesses, and geographies increasingly encounter complexities that threaten their success. A common response is to set up control systems— reports, measures, and rewards—that inhibit the very results intended. This happens when we violate natural laws, inhibit free flow of information, and impose unnecessary constraints. These external forces tend to drive out people's natural motivation.

In contrast, taming the chaos and managing complexity are possible when stakeholders establish a strong sense of purpose, develop shared vision and values, share information as an enabling factor, and adopt patterns that promote cooperation across cultural boundaries. These processes represent major changes for many organizations. They also constitute the means to lead with power.

Too late, people often learn the power of a nonguiding coalition. This happens when a surprise attack results in a resource getting pulled, a project manager is reassigned, or a project is cancelled. Getting explicit commitments up front, the more public the better, is important to implementing any project or initiative. It also takes follow-through to maintain the commitment. But if commitment was not obtained initially, it is not possible to maintain throughout. It all starts by investigating attitudes and assessing how things get done.

## Views of Politics

It is said that Albert Einstein once observed that "politics is more difficult than physics." Politics will be present anytime an attempt is made to turn a vision for change into reality. It is a fact of life, not a dirty word that should be stamped out. A common view is what happens with negative politics, which is a win-lose environment in an underhanded or without-your-knowledge-of-what's-happening approach. People feel manipulated, and the outcome is not desirable from their point of view. Secret discussions are more prevalent than public ones. Reciprocal agreements are made to benefit individuals rather than organizations.

Project managers and sponsors who shy away from power and politics are not being all they can be. A big pitfall for people is not taking the time to fully assess what they are up against—learning how to operate effectively in a political environment.

What is a political environment? A negative reaction to the word *political* could be a barrier to success. Being political is not a bad thing when trying to get good things done for the organization. A political environment is the power structure, formal and informal. It is how things get done in the day-to-day processes as well as in a network of relationships. Power is the capacity each individual possesses to translate intention into reality and sustain it. Organizational politics is the exercise or use of power. Since project management is all about getting results, it stands to reason that power is required. Political savvy is a vital ingredient for every sponsor's toolkit.

The political process is always at work in organizations. The political jungle is a chaotic environment. Success comes to those who identify the "animals" in the jungle and recognize that they exhibit certain traits and patterns. Each is driven by a purpose. Being effective with the "lions, tigers, and bears" involves working in their preferred operating modes, speaking their language, and aligning common purposes.

The challenge is to create an environment for positive politics. In a positive political environment, people operate with a win-win attitude. All actions are out in the open. People demonstratively work hard toward the common good. Outcomes are desirable or at least acceptable to all parties concerned. Good, smart people who trust each other (even if they do not always agree), getting together to solve clearly defined and important issues, guided by effective, facilitated processes, with full disclosure and all information out in the open, can accomplish almost anything. This is the view of power and politics that we espouse.

## Assessing the Political Environment

Understand the power structure in the organization. A view from outer space would not show the lines that separate countries or organizations or functional areas or political boundaries. The lines are artificial figments that exist in our minds or on paper but not in physical reality. Clues to a power structure may come from an organizational chart, but how things get done goes far beyond that. Influence exists in people's hearts and minds, where power derives more from legitimacy than from authority. Its presence occurs in the implementation of decisions.

Legitimacy is what people confer on their leaders. Being authentic and acting with integrity are factors a leader decides in relations to others, and legitimacy is the response from others. Position power may command respect, but ultimately how a leader behaves is what gains wholehearted commitment from followers. Legitimacy is the real prize, for it completes the circle. When people accept and legitimize the power of a leader, greater support gets directed toward the outcome; conversely, less resistance is present.

People have always used organizations to amplify human power. Art Kleiner (2003) states a premise that in every organization there is a core group of key people—the "people who really matter"—in which the organization continually acts to fulfill the perceived needs and priorities of this group.

Kleiner suggests numerous ways to determine who these powerful people are. People who have power are at the center of the organization's informal network. They are symbolic representatives of the organization's direction. They got this way because of their position, their rank, their ability to hire and fire others. Maybe they control a key bottleneck or belong to a particular influential subculture. They may have personal charisma or integrity. These people take a visible stand on behalf of the organization's principles and engender a level of mutual respect. They dedicate themselves as leaders to the organization's ultimate best interests and set the organization's direction. As they think or act or convey an attitude, so does the rest of the organization. Their characteristics and principles convey what an organization stands for. These are key people who, when open to change, can influence an organization to move in new directions or, when not open to change, keep it the same.

Another way to recognize key people is to look for decision makers in the mainstream business of the organization. They may be aligned with the headquarters culture, ethnic basis, or gender; speak the native language; or be part of the founding family. Some questions to ask about people in the organization are these: Whose interests did we consider in making a decision? Who gets things done? Who could stop something from happening? Who are the "heroes"?

Power is not imposed by boundaries. Power is earned, not demanded. Power can come from position in the organization, what a person knows, a network of relationships, and possibly from the situation, meaning that a person could be placed in a situation that has a great deal of importance and focus at that moment.

A simple test for where power and influence reside is to observe whom people talk to or go to with questions or for advice. Whose desk do people meet at? Who always complains about a long string of voice or e-mail messages? Whose calendar is hard to get onto?

One of the most reliable sources of power when working across organizations is the credibility a sponsor builds through a network of relationships. It is necessary to have credibility before a person can attract team members, especially the best people, who are usually busy and have many other things competing for their time. Credibility comes from building relationships in a political environment.

In contrast, credibility gaps occur when prior experience did not fulfill expectations or when perceived abilities to perform are unknown and therefore questionable. Organizational memory has a lingering effect—people long remember what happened before and do not give up these perceptions without due cause. People more easily align with someone who has the power of knowledge credibility.

Power and politics also address the basic priority of project management's triple constraints—outcome, schedule, and cost. If the power in an organization resides in marketing where trade shows rule new product introductions, meeting market window schedules becomes most important. An R&D-driven organization tends to focus on features and new technology, often at the expense of schedule and cost.

## Mapping Behavior

Stakeholder analysis is integral to a political plan. One format is to apply traits or characteristics of animals to people in the organization. Our experience demonstrates that it is a fun and less risky approach to sensitive topics. People quickly come to understand the challenges of dealing with these "animals."

For example, assess each individual for the degree of mutual trust and for agreement on the project or program's purpose, vision, and mission. That puts each person in one of four quadrants. Identify what sort of "animal" the person is and position him or her on the grid. Here are some examples:

*Tiger:* Solitary, powerful, strong, and skillful

*Lion:* Social, outgoing, approachable, loud

*Bear:* Solitary, intelligent, avoidant of people

*Venomous snake:* Cold-blooded, ruthless when provoked

*Female black widow spider:* Shy and solitary but poisonous; willing to devour weaker colleagues

*Arctic fox:* Easy to recognize but hard to catch; smiling but manipulative

*Raccoon:* Intensely curious

*Sheep:* Dependent on the herd; willing to follow leaders and produce whatever is required

Ultimately, the goal is to move everyone up and to the right on the stakeholder grid in Figure 10.1. This grid is a stakeholder analysis tool that combines diagnoses about mutual trust, agreement on purpose, vision, mission, and "political jungle" characteristics to assess the current environment and then develop an approach to each stakeholder. Moving everyone up and to the right is the most productive situation when surrounded by allies. Those in the opponents quadrant need attention to build agreement. Those on the left side need trust building. The "animals" describe the personal characteristics that need to be considered when deciding a course of action with each stakeholder to ensure support for a project. Start by reinforcing positions of strength, and then work on areas of concern. Use the knowledge about traits and behavior patterns to address each stakeholder's needs, as well as to protect yourself when necessary.

With these concepts in minds, the next task for the project leader is to apply political savvy in the organizational environment. Difficult challenges that arise do not have simple answers, but effective action can be guided by applying the concepts of authenticity

**Figure 10.1  Stakeholder Grid**

and integrity. These are fundamental concepts that get left out of modern business activities. We may be tempted or pressured by short-term expedient responses. However, imagine yourself five years in the future looking back on this time. What will you be most proud of? What will you remember—that you met a budget or did the right thing?

For example, it is easy to get caught in a vicious loop when there is no time to create a clear and widely understood business vision—daily actions consist of problem solving and firefighting, often driven more by urgency than by importance. Consequently, work is not consistent prioritized, and the vast diversity of job concerns leaves even less time for reflection on levels of importance. Choices are made in isolation, leading to duplication of effort or gaps in the product line. This ultimately produces unsatisfactory business results because the important things do not get done. We then come full circle around the loop to need a clear business vision. The trick is to break the loop somewhere.

Leaders, caught up in a vicious loop like the one in Figure 10.2 and speaking without authenticity and committing integrity crimes, shift the burden in the wrong direction. Leaders have a choice: to ignore fundamental values and get into a difficult predicament or to tap the energy and loyalty of others to help everyone succeed. The difference resides in authenticity and integrity.

In the discipline of systems thinking, this predicament is a classic example of a "shifting the burden" archetype. Such an archetype is a pattern that helps explain recurring behaviors in human interactions. Shifting the burden occurs when applying a short-term fix actually undermines a leader's ability to take action at a more fundamental level. The causal loop, starting in the middle of Figure 10.3, depicts how many project leaders proceed when under pressure to get results. The quick fix (in balancing loop B1) is to resort to a command-and-control approach, which on a surface level appears to lessen the pressure. However, this approach drives individuals to commit integrity crimes when they believe that what they say is more important than what they do. This has an opposite

## Figure 10.2   The Vicious Loop of Ignored Fundamental Values

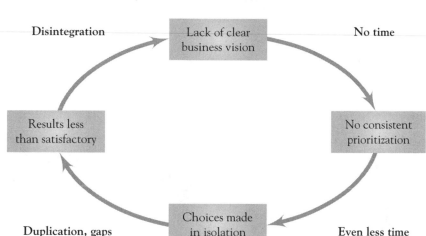

effect on the people they want to influence or persuade (in reinforcing loop R3). These people do not do their best work, placing more pressure on getting results.

The top loop is the common situation that leads to getting worse and is the single loop that people get stuck in. The bottom or double loop is a corrective action to do something fundamentally different. The outer loop is a common solution that just leads to getting worse. We need to understand cause-and-effect relationships, break the loop somewhere (often it does not matter exactly where), and do something different. The new actions cannot help but lead to change because that is the nature of cause and effect. The good news about his approach is to avoid being overwhelmed by the political environment and to take small actions that may have more favorable outcomes because you understand the natural cycles affecting all that we do.

Feedback is a powerful tool to guide behavior. Mapping behaviors shows how what we do comes back to help or hurt us. It also shows the ripple effect of multiple actions—in other words, how interdependent we are. These tools reinforce the need to be careful in what we do when interacting with others and also the power of

## Figure 10.3 Shifting-the-Burden Archetype

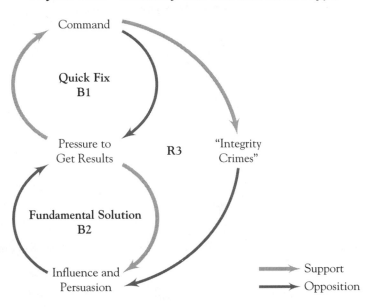

changing behaviors by giving feedback to others about possible consequences of their actions. This leads to self-correcting behaviors.

Know also that leadership, and subsequent followership, depends on the emotional bonding and alignment that occurs among people, teams, and the organization. This becomes a primary role for leading in a political environment—developing skills of emotional intelligence and practicing "primal leadership" (Goleman, Boyatzis, and McKee, 2002). A sponsor's goal is to grow capacity in people and the organization. This means support the extent that people have the intellectual, emotional, physical, and financial resources necessary to adjust to necessary changes. It may mean dropping old beliefs and behaviors; do this through open discussions where people come to value the new rather than hanging on to the old.

The fundamental solution to the pressure to get results is to develop skills of persuasion as practiced by a change agent (in balancing loop B2). Help people believe in the vision and mission and also help them figure out why it is in their best interest to put their best work into the project. People usually respond positively to this approach and accomplish the work with less pressure. Tap people's innate talents, and create a natural environment where thoughts and information move freely. This virtuous loop represents a political plan at its finest.

## Authentic Leadership in Action

A fundamental solution to creating a political plan includes applying tools of influence and persuasion such as the following:

- *Reciprocity.* Give an unsolicited gift. People will feel the need to give something back. Perhaps a big contract or maybe another opportunity to continue building a strong relationship.

- *Consistency.* Draw people into public commitments, even very small ones. This can be very effective in directing future action. Ask for explicit commitments, and enforce them consistently.

- *Social validation.* Let people know that implementing a project management methodology is considered the standard by others. People often determine what they should do by looking at what others are doing.

- *Liking.* Let people know that you like them and that you are likable too. People like to do business with people they like. Elements that build liking include physical attractiveness, similarity, compliments, and cooperation.

- *Authority.* Be professional and personable. A suit and tie can do wonders. Other factors are experience, expertise, and scientific credentials. Tap referential power by being publicly named as the program sponsor by someone high up in the organization; use that connection to get the attention of others.

- *Scarcity.* Notice just how rare good program practice is, not to mention people who can transform a culture. Not everyone knows what it takes to make a program successful. Stand out as a person who is willing to do the right things in the right ways.

Cialdini (2000) sums up the science and practice of persuasion like this: repay favors, behave consistently, follow the lead of similar others, favor the requests of those we like, heed legitimate authorities, and value scare resources.

Creating an environment for successful projects means that all players, and especially sponsors, act with authenticity and integrity. Authenticity means that people believe what they say. Integrity means that they do what they say they will do, and for the reasons they stated to begin with. Authenticity and integrity link the head and the heart, the words and the action; they separate belief from disbelief and often make the difference between success and failure. Many people in organizations lament that their leaders lack authenticity and integrity. When that feeling is prevalent, trust cannot develop, and optimal results are difficult if not impossible to achieve (Graham and Englund, 2004).

Integrity is the most difficult—and the most important—value a leader can demonstrate. Integrity is revealed slowly, day by day, in word and deed. Actions that compromise a leader's integrity often have swift and profound repercussions. Every leader is in the spotlight of the people they lead. As a result, shortcomings in integrity are readily apparent. Political leaders who failed often did so not by their deeds but by integrity gaps.

Here are some guidelines for achieving integrity:

- Identify basic leadership traits and their consequences; know yourself.
- Assess and compare leadership approaches in complex situations; practice developing judgment by simulating what you would do and comparing that to what respected leaders actually did.
- Break the vicious loop somewhere; then modify a burden-shifting structure to create a positive culture.
- Appreciate the value of authentic leadership, and commit to act with integrity.

It becomes painfully evident when team members sense a disconnect between what they and their sponsor believe is important. Energy levels drop, and productive work either ceases or slows down.

Sponsors who commit integrity crimes (some examples are given in Exhibit 10.1) display aspects of a common challenge—becoming a victim of the measurement and reward system. "Show me how people are measured," the axiom holds, "and I'll show you how they behave." People have inner voices that reflect values and beliefs that lead to authenticity and integrity. They also experience external pressures to get results. The test for a true leader is to balance the internal with external pressures and to demonstrate truthfulness so that all concerned come to believe in the direction chosen. Know that people will generally work anytime and follow anywhere a person who leads with authenticity and integrity. Be that person. Measurement systems need to reflect authentically on the values and guiding principles of the organization. Forced or misguided metrics and rewards do more harm than good. Unrealistic deadlines with no obvious motivation are deadly. Be aware of unintended consequences. Unattended consequences occur when shooting from the hip without considering a more systematic approach to

### Exhibit 10.1  Violations of Integrity: Some Examples

- A sponsor giving a pep talk to the project team on the unrealistic "merits" of doing an eighteen-month project in six months
- Starting a meeting with a stated intention but diverting it to meet another assignment
- Passing along to the rank and file senior management statements that the speaker is not in agreement with
- Ending telephone conversations with "Someone's at my desk so I have to go now"
- Requiring weekly milestones to be met and promising feedback and customer reviews but not providing it
- Directing that a new standard methodology be used but not training people to use it
- Promising a contract for the following week but not sending it

any situation—you solve the current problem but create other problems. Sponsors may set up metrics, rewards, or reporting requirements so that they can feel comfortable about what is going on but do not realize how others react who get a message that they are not trusted to do the right thing. Another example is marketing messages that do not translate well or when translated mean something derogatory.

## Preparing a Political Plan

The concepts discussed in this chapter can be recorded on a form or template like the sample shown in Exhibit 10.2. Record your reflections on the culture, prior behaviors, and recurring issues. Think about creating small wins that set the stage for broader-based actions across the organization. Decide on a role, and prepare to take action.

### Exhibit 10.2  A Sample Political Plan

**Assessment of the Environment**

*We are a "loose-tight" organization with a moderately weak project culture. Power is relatively diffused, and no one person dominates team meetings. People with initiative can step up and succeed, but few of these efforts are coordinated across the organization. Ineffective and inefficient processes are a big problem.*

**Description of the Political Jungle**

*The tigers stay out of our way. The lions roars are not heard very far, and the bears seem to run the show, doing their own thing. Venomous attacks can come from anywhere, especially when traversing new territories.*

**Stakeholder Roles**

*Sponsors are assigned but do not actively support projects unless asked. Team members lack full commitment to the project because of other distractions. Senior management is just beginning to understand the value of project and program management to the vitality of the organization.*

## Exhibit 10.2  A Sample Political Plan, Cont'd

### Potential Issues

*Too many projects threatens successful completion. Requirements change when managers cater to special interests. Vague understanding of roles and responsibilities creates confusion and leads to missed milestones. Few commitments exist to follow through on project plans.*

### Approach to Stakeholders and Issues

*Need to get tigers involved in supporting program management and a project portfolio process. Need to harness the lions to roar in concert by focusing on a limited set of strategic goals and corresponding projects. The bears will continue to perform as long as we do not disturb them too greatly with complex processes or detailed checklists.*

### Strategic Responses (Positions, Steps to Take)

*A small project office reporting to the general manager can facilitate the introduction of simple portfolio and project management processes. Get the attention of the lions by pointing out the consequences in the market if we fail to coordinate our efforts systematically. Neutralize negative behaviors by taking an open approach to all issues and the free flow of information.*

### Action Plans

- *Interview all stakeholders.*
- *Prepare a proposal.*
- *Line up upper management support.*
- *Define the project sponsor role and conduct training for new sponsors.*
- *Develop an environment where excellence in project sponsorship contributes to competitive advantage.*
- *Select strategic efforts leading first to small wins before rolling out more broadly.*
- *Get explicit commitments from all stakeholders.*
- *Remember to be authentic and act with integrity on every interaction.*

Approach organizational politics like a chess game. You are aware of the role and power of each chess piece, but success in the game depends on your movements and the movements of your adversary. Sponsors and project managers need to be good chess players because that way they will be able to influence people in organizations. One of us (Bucero) discovered the similarities between a project and a chess game on a recent vacation. My eight-year-old son knew how to identify who has the power in each movement and was able to use it. Sometimes he failed; sometimes he succeeded. That is a typical scenario.

## Summary

This chapter focuses on project reviews and operating in a political environment. Supporting knowledge management processes and taking action on continuous learning is most effectively accomplished in the sponsorship role. Many organizations lack good political "swimmers." Leading with power is a learned skill. It involves assessment, identification, skill building, planning, and application. Like all learning, it involves movement between reflection and action.

Creating a political plan starts with making a commitment to lead with power, most probably personal power. It continues by identifying sources of power, performing stakeholder analysis, and applying the values of authenticity and integrity. Look systematically at the environment, which may be depicted as a vicious loop. Instead, create a virtuous loop based on tools of persuasion and influence. Trust cannot develop and even quests to implement enterprise project management remain a fiction until leaders create an environment that supports these qualities. Take the time to document a political plan, noting your observations and deciding on action steps.

## Some Closing Thoughts

This book is all about achieving better results from project-based work. Our objective is to convey that excellence in sponsorship plays a major role in optimizing outcomes. A sponsor initiates, funds, and supports the project from its inception through its completion and on throughout the project outcome life cycle. Proactive sponsorship is the ideal. Selecting the right people, clarifying roles, making the commitment, and getting appropriate training are steps along the path. Managers acting as project sponsors need to spend time with every project team member, dealing with misunderstandings and varying perceptions. Sustaining energy is also required.

Many other sponsorship roles may accrue, be cast on, or come from enlightened persons who find creative ways to express leadership and make a contribution. Mentoring accelerates this process; in fact, coaching and mentoring are desired characteristics of a good sponsor. A key obligation of the project sponsor is to create the right environment for project success. Achieving excellence in sponsorship means that senior managers get to maintain a hands-off approach but are available when problems come up.

Success starts with a strong commitment to improve. Leaders become better prepared as sponsors of major projects by taking inventory of their talents, skills, and behaviors and putting appropriate action plans in place. Knowledge management encompasses the ascent from data to information to knowledge and wisdom. Reaching the top of the stairway represents enlightenment—eyes are fully open about why, what, and how to invoke excellence in project sponsorship.

An objective for this book is to unlock and open the door of sponsorship. The reader has choices: ignore the opportunities the open door represents, approach it cautiously, or pass through it eagerly. As you stand before an open door, you can spend time and energy on non-value-adding activities—or embrace sponsor and management commitments that achieve project success. Executives need training, experience, and practice to be effective sponsors. Sponsorship is a required and critical success factor for all projects, in all industries and disciplines. Move forward, because every day is a good day for change.

Figure 10.4 summarizes the content of this book in a mind map. Use this map as a quick-reference guide, both for this book and in practice.

## Figure 10.4  Mind Map of the Content of This Book

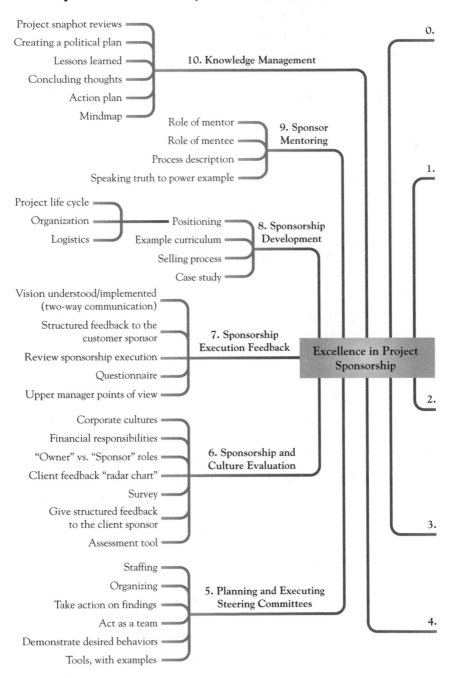

# Figure 10.4 Mind Map of the Content of This Book, Cont'd

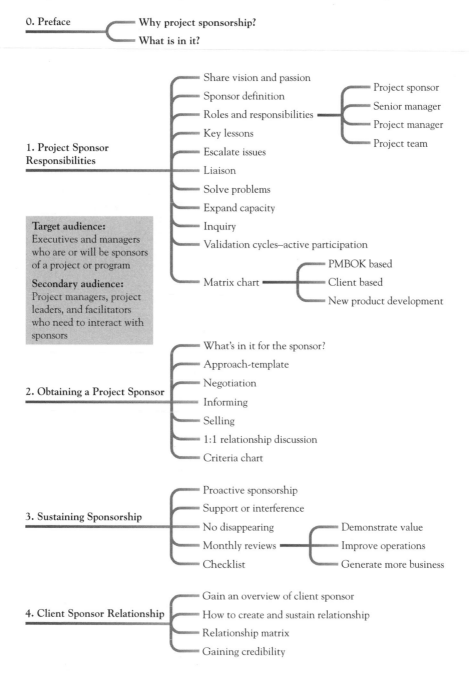

# Bibliography

Belluzzo, R. E. "How to Manage, Lead, and Succeed." Presentation at Get Motivated Seminars, 2003, pp. 30–31.

Bucero, A. "How to Manage the Change Through Project Management: Red Castle Project—A Real Case." Paper presented at the World Project Management Week conference, Cairns, Australia, Oct. 10, 2000.

Bucero, A. "Forging the Future Through PMO Implementation: A Case Study of Sponsorship." Paper presented at the Project Management Institute's European Project Management Conference, Cannes, France, June 20, 2002a.

Bucero, A. "Improving Performance Through the PMO: A Real Case." Symposium presented at the International Public Management Association's Project Management Conference, Berlin, Germany, June 2002b.

Cialdini, R. B. *Influence: Science and Practice.* (4th ed.) Boston: Allyn & Bacon, 2000.

Conner, D. R. *Managing at the Speed of Change.* New York: Random House, 1993.

Cooke-Davies, T. J. "The Executive Sponsor: The Hinge upon Which Organisational Project Management Maturity Turns?" Paper presented at the Project Management Institute's Global Congress, Edinburgh, Scotland, May 24, 2005.

Englund, R. L. "Authenticity and Integrity." *PM Network,* Aug. 2000.

Englund, R. L. *Environmental Assessment Survey Instrument.* 2004a. [http://www. englundpmc.com; "Offerings"].

Englund, R. L. "Leading with Power." Paper presented at the Project Management Institute's Global Congress 2004, North America, Anaheim, California, Oct. 25, 2004b.

Englund, R. L., Graham, R. J., and Dinsmore, P. C. *Creating the Project Office: A Manager's Guide to Leading Organizational Change.* San Francisco: Jossey-Bass, 2003.

Goleman, D., Boyatzis, R., and McKee, A. *Primal Leadership: Realizing the Power of Emotional Intelligence.* Boston: Harvard Business School Press, 2002.

Görög, M., and Smith, N. J. *Project Management for Managers.* Newtown Square, Pa.: Project Management Institute, 1999.

Graham, R. J., and Englund, R. L. *Creating an Environment for Successful Projects.* (2nd ed.) San Francisco: Jossey-Bass, 2004.

Greenleaf, R. K. *Servant Leadership: A Journey into the Nature of Legitimate Power and Greatness.* Mahwah, N.J.: Paulist Press, 1977.

Hall, P. "CIOs Can't Do It Alone: Project Success Through Better Sponsorship." *Cutter IT Journal,* Aug. 2003, pp 8–12.

Harris, P. R., and Moran, R. T. *Managing Cultural Differences.* Houston, Tex.: Gulf, 1996.

Holmes, A. "The Four (Not Three, Not Five) Principles of Managing Expectations." *CIO.* Nov. 1, 2005, pp. 59–66.

Kendall, G. L., and Rollins, S. C. *Advanced Project Portfolio Management and the PMO: Multiplying ROI at Warp Speed.* Fort Lauderdale, Fla.: Ross, 2003.

Kendrick, T. *Identifying and Managing Project Risk: Essential Tools for Failure-Proofing Your Project.* New York: AMACOM, 2003.

Kleiner, A. *Who Really Matters: The Core Group Theory of Power, Privilege, and Success.* New York: Currency Doubleday, 2003.

Kouzes, J. M., and Posner, B. Z. *Credibility: How Leaders Gain and Lose It, Why People Demand It.* San Francisco: Jossey-Bass, 1993.

Liegel, K. "Q and A Creative Calls: What Is the Most Creative Leadership Decision You Have Ever Made?" *PM Network,* May 2005, pp. 642–663.

Love, N., and Brant-Love, J. *The Project Sponsor Guide.* Newtown Square, Pa.: Project Management Institute, 2000.

McKenzie, R. *The Relationship-Based Enterprise: Powering Business Success Through Customer Relationship Management.* New York: McGraw-Hill, 2001.

Morris, P.W.G. "Managing the Front End: How Project Managers Shape Business Strategy and Manage Project Definition." Paper presented at the Project Management Institute's Global Congress, Edinburgh, Scotland, May 24, 2005.

O'Connor, P. "Aligning, Integrating, and Facilitating: Doubling NPD Output." A periodic newsletter from Paul O'Connor, NPDP (www.adept-plm.com), Jan. 11, 2006.

Pacelli, L. "Top Ten Attributes of a Great Project Sponsor." Paper presented at the Project Management Institute's Global Congress, North America 2005, Toronto, Canada, Sept. 12, 2005.

Pinto, J. K *Power and Politics in Project Management.* Newtown Square, Pa.: Project Management Institute, 1996.

Project Management Institute. *A Guide to the Project Management Body of Knowledge.* (3rd ed.) Newtown Square, Pa.: Project Management Institute, 2004.

Senge, P. M., and others. *The Fifth Discipline Fieldbook.* New York: Doubleday/Currency, 1994.

Senge, P. M., and others. *The Dance of Change: The Challenges to Sustaining Momentum in Learning Organizations.* New York: Doubleday/Currency, 1999.

Strategic Management Group. *Understanding Project Management*. CD-ROM. Conshohocken, Pa.: Strategic Management Group, n.d.

Thomas, J., Delisle, C. L., and Jugdev, K. *Selling Project Management to Senior Executives: Framing the Moves That Matter*. Newtown Square, Pa.: Project Management Institute, 2002.

Urban, C. "The Human Factor of Change Management." *Training*, Dec. 22, 2004. [http://www.trainingmag.com/training/reports_analysis/feature_display.jsp?vnu_content_id=1000709589].

Verma, V. K. *Organizing Projects for Success: The Human Aspects of Project Management*. Newtown Square, Pa.: Project Management Institute, 1995.

Young, A. *The Manager's Handbook: The Practical Illustrated Guide to Successful Management*. New York: Crown, 1986.

# Index